To gentleman Jeff

I hope you will enjoy both a bit
of the Maltese touch in this book
and my humble journey.

Growing with the Shadows

Enjoy, God bless

Your Maltese Falcon.

Ray

GROWING
with the
SHADOWS

Poems By

Dr. RAYMOND FENECH

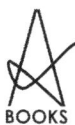

Adelaide Books
New York / Lisbon

2018

Growing with the Shadows
A Collection of Poems
By Dr. Raymond Fenech

Published by Adelaide Books, New York / Lisbon

Cover design & Interior Formatting:
Adelaide Books DBA, New York

Editor-in-Chief
Stevan V. Nikolic

For any information, please contact Adelaide Books
at info@adelaidebooks.org
or write to
Adelaide Books
244 Fifth Avenue, Suite D27
New York, NY, 10001

ISBN13: 978-1-7320742-8-6
ISBN10: 1-7320742-8-3

Printed in the United States of America

Dedicated to my wife Angela,

who has stood by me for thirty-two years through shine, rain and storm. She has been my inspiration and more important than that, my motivation to pursue my writing career, which from the very commencement when I was thirteen, proved one of the most arduous challenges in my life. Her continuous support and encouragement, even when my work looked clearly destined to remain unpublished and unread was a stupendous feat of courage and a 'Never say die' attitude only she could have summed up in such hostile conditions; even when I was battling cancer lymphoma. Thank you Angela for being the love and light of my life, my soul mate, and my most treasured and faithful companion.

"Keep in mind how fast things pass by and are gone–those that are now and those to come. Existence flows past us like a river: the 'what' is in constant flux, the 'why' has a thousand variations. Nothing is stable, not even what's right here. The infinity of past and future gapes before us–a chasm whose depths we cannot see." (Marcus Aurelius)

Contents

IMAGINATION DREAMS & FANTASY

SHORT POEMS

Introduction

TIME-TRAVELLING
WITH RAYMOND FENECH

A Review by Prof. Miguel Ángel Olivé Iglesias
Associate Professor at Holoquin University, Cuba

Richard Marvin Grove, Founder and President of the Canada Cuba Literary Alliance (CCLA), asked me to review a book of poetry by Dr Raymond Fenech, a CCLA member and outstanding writer and poet. From Fenech´s impressive biography and personal comments, I already had extra glimpses into his life and his work. In my review of this book, every single poem was a joy to read but I have highlighted what I deemed to be some of the best poems by the author. I'll leave the others for the readers to judge.

In my initial reading of *Growing With the Shadows* , most of all I visualized a man of infinite suffering, greatly affected by Life or Death, nonetheless without losing hope and that ceaseless struggle towards the light. As Pablo Neruda, the great Chilean poet, said: "They tell me: you belong in the shadows. Perhaps, perhaps, but I walk towards the light" [1].

Many times, Fenech is a man bordering on the grim reaper's realm, yet also a concerned environmentalist worried about the relentless action of his fellow men against nature and the conservation of places, as well as the lost values, both material and spiritual. He shows

himself to the world as a down-to-earth time traveler who seeks peace and an escape valve in his naturalistic, soaring poetry that I now compare to his own simile in one of his Tanka poems, *Waves* "like a brandished scimitar".

I was enraptured by Fenech's poems because he took me on a time traveling experience at roller-coaster speed. A cursory read of the book would lead any impromptu reader to want to separate some poems from others but after you read them all, you realize that it cannot be done: the poems stand and flare on their own right as a necessary and sweeping monolithic comet. They belong with each other, and with the author. Each seems to have been carved with Fenech's blood, entrails and experiences of a sensitive poet slit by what he sees and feels, and his need to display things as they are, crude and raw, presenting characters and events as they happened.

The Dream and the Glory, is a poem where the poet is loyal to his principles of writing (present in all his work): "I like to write poetry in a language everyone can understand, without mincing words, or losing my way in the obscure, or the abstract [2]". There is so much crushing truth in the rhetorical questions that close the poem. The poet is visionary revealing his objectivity in his writing, maybe also his pessimism tinted by the harrowing predicaments in his life. Yet as a reader, I could also sense renewed strength in him and a breath of optimism in having defeated the ghosts that stalked him, a recurring theme in his book, when he says that he is both "aloof and alert". His refuge in the past he loved comes back as a warning of the futility of things like glory, a topic re-visited in his other poem, Tempus Fugit.

This Will Never happen to me Syndrome is a narration written by the author when he was diagnosed with Cancer Lymphoma. The poem is oozing with pain, but

optimism is discernible in this tour-de-force experimental poem. Fenech voices that "Now I stand again" and skillfully displays his strongly descriptive metaphors, similes and literary allusions when he shouts that, "So I will call out my fearsome 300 Spartans to turn this scuffle into a last spectacular tussle" thus showing clearly he won't surrender.

To Sadness returns to the happy memories the author is so adhered to. The poem confronts sadness and talks to it face to face. Ray's, *The Mannequin* is a wonderfully knitted piece that unveils a contrast between the stripped bare, the deadly and the author's capability of seeing the poetic side of the situation then falling in love. *The Vampire* is like a film, where Fenech X-rays the psychology of the vampire along with the human's. The phrase "For he fears humans more than humans fear him" is lapidary and understandable as the reader treks into the next three lines...

Light after Dark is a poem where brightness and optimism vibrate and bring comfort to the reader – intermittently. There are again expressive means and stylistic devices, metaphors and similes, masterfully handled by the poet: "moon-filled pond" got to me, as did "cut by a sword that flashes in the night". This is not trite imagery, it dwells inside the poet, and he is disposed to share it with his readers. "And we can see with touch" is another superb line in this poem, which reminded me of Shakespeare's "To hear with eyes belongs to love's fine wit" [3]. Both poets play with the senses, a sleight of hand of vision, hearing and touching.

Platonic Love is great storytelling; Fenech remains faithful to his direct-language style without relinquishing his tropes and images. The poet ends the poem with "A love so perfect, it could not survive". The phrase is an antithesis, he elaborates on the notion of perfection, a

moving target difficult to reach, either in the mind or at a social level. In many ways, I see irony underneath the story, fleeting limitations of human love, but also a tweak at a society he criticizes.

The poem, *Fleur* discloses the learning of the facts of life where love and sex are depicted here. Pablo Neruda comes to my mind again with his poems about puberty, teen age, youth and the discovery of sex and beauty when he was young: "I felt something changed inside me, an electric flower, the hungry and pure flower of desire [4]". I take my hat off to both Neruda and Fenech. This theme is repeated in other poems, such as: *Our Maid Claire.* Along with the issue of love and sex, Fenech points at society and the prejudices rising above his epoch – something we will see soar to environmentalist maturity in his poetry: "We lived in an unforgiving world that discriminates between race and class. Claire was just our maid".

Forbidden Love and *Endless Summers* are both love poems filled with throat-cutting and exquisite phrases so like Fenech´s style – phrases prudish readers might consider too brash. Metaphors and similes refresh the reader's expectations. In the former, it remains to explore why that love was forbidden, in the latter similes embrace the eye: "like fired mirrors", "like an indelible portrait", etc.

The Bridge brings sweet pain, as much an oxymoron as my phrase is the very mental frame Fenech depicts, succeeding to sketch in the contrasts that fuse time and space. There are many meanings to that bridge, one of them provided by the environmentalist and social critic, so concerned about what is happening with development and concrete replacing the old houses.

The Swing in the Garden is a to and fro nostalgic swaying of the poet's reminiscences. It is a wistful poem, full of pictorial messages, nicely embroidered

with onomatopoeias (tick-tocking, choochoo) and enjoyable rhyme like many other poems in the book. One can almost hear the rusty, frictional sound of the swing propped by the words, creaking, screeching, excruciating, sound combinations known as indirect onomatopoeias. Edgar Allan Poe would have loved it! ("And the silken, sad, uncertain rustling of each purple curtain" [5]).

Tempus Fugit is an ode to time. Once more Shakespeare is paid homage to: some of his recurring themes were death and immortality bring to mind, Sonnets XIX ("Devouring Time"), CXVI ("Within his (Time's) bending sickle's compass come"), among others. Time is personified, a resource that brings it closer to our comprehension of the author's anguish and state of mind.

The Bird of Paradise offers epigrammatic lines, a virtue that must be a natural rule in good poetry and highlighted by the line, "It matters how we live, not how we die". Fenech retakes his ideas about glory and the futility of it all when he closes the poem: "Like human glory – the ever deluding myth".

In The Waiting Room, Fenech appropriates himself of time and the past and depicts human behaviour through two main characters, (secretary and lawyer), but makes reference as well to people in general. Metaphors, "Time screeches away the centuries", similes "like the curtains on a stage, "files like tombstones" and an onomatopoeia like "tick tock" complement in displaying the mood of the scene.

The Glory and the Strife proposes rhetorical questions: "Are we really here, did we live this life…" that are instantly replied to with what I dare call "rhetorical-question answers": "… Or is all forgotten, the glory and the strife?" These refer once more to his

constant queries about glory, oblivion and the futility of life.

A Sonnet with Some Advice returns to how fast life flies. Epigrammatic lines captured me: "Except your smile and let God take the lead". The first time Fenech mentions God is to deny Him (*The Dream and the Glory*); now he goes back to God, to acknowledge Him. Still in the cord of seeking refuge in the past and in his childhood moments, Fenech sounds less pessimistic in this poem, but probably because it was one of his earlier works.

The Dandelion Seed is a very powerful poem. Its last two lines are epigrams on their own right: "Within this seed there is no pain of birth / at death it simply turns to dust". Calm appreciation of the poet where he seems to wish he was that seed, but from a philosophical abstraction that seems not to hurt him. Poppies are not even in Dreams shows the heart of a true green regaling us with lines that are prophetic: "The sun is no longer visible as it sets behind the high-rise buildings", "Soon these poppies will not even be in their dreams".

In *A Mosquito's buzzing Birth*, Fenech uses onomatopoeia in combined orchestration of buzzing, azure, razzing, fizzed, dazed, dazzled, jazz, zigzagged, zipped, zapped, blaze, buzz. Well, you can actually hear the acute buzzing sound of the mosquito!

In *Apocalypse*, the poet warns of the danger of devastating the world's natural landscapes and seas. This is not just a poet's claim; it is scientifically proven. Nature will take a deadly toll on humans as retaliation for the harm inflicted on the environment. Onomatopoeia once more contributes to perk the senses of the reader with a deluge of words: whines, whooshes, whips, bashing, crush, blushing.

Roller Skating down Memory Lane is a trip where time and space fuse in the author's nostalgia. He

introduces a mighty stylistic device, foreignism; that is chiefly used to convey the poet's desired effects on the reader, by placing here and there words or phrases that colour the scenarios being described. It brings the reader to the contexts depicted, enriches the ideas with touches of the atmosphere that is best represented by interspersing Maltese words such as 'luzzi'. The taste then is different, more in line with the story being told and the culture being photographed. What mostly captivated me, though, were two lines that speak highly of Fenech's ideology and values: "cars, designers' clothes and fashion were not important as people's feelings, family values and virtues". Fenech is an inveterate advocate of goodness, and a convinced dreamer. John Lennon's, *Imagine* translated into poetry.

The use of Maltese words is abundant in *Sunrise of a Fishing Village*. The reader is immersed in the actual world that is laid down for him/her. Irony, as a stylistic device too, is felt in these lines. The moral stature of Fenech and his awareness of the poet's role cannot be questioned: "Who cares about politicians and their lies? Who cares about all those self centred snobs who have never seen Pawlu's fresh lampuki?" Again Fenech is mirrored in Neruda's words: "My duties walk side by side with my voice" and "I am the man of bread and fish... you will find me among women and men [6]". The nostalgic lover of nature is highlighted with the words, "The fresh smell of the sea and the salt".

Paul the Meticulous Fisherman is a repository of foreignisims that enhance the message of the poem. Questions are left to dangle in the air about what happens. The mysteries of life and the quirks of fate take hold of the reader. *The Vegetable and Fruit Vendor* is storytelling that recreates life in the fishing village. Well narrated, sad and inquisitive of destiny and death. *The Last Apassionata to my Mother* is a beautiful ode to the

poet's late mother. It is bordered with constant allusions to music classics, Mozart, Beethoven, Bach. Fenech finds shelter in memories of his mother and his childhood: "my refuge for decades from spring to the fall".

Straw Hat is a fine melancholic poem that praises the sentimental value of things, a virtue lost today. Strong personification (or perhaps, "animalization" of the wind) and intertwining similes: "Winds will howl... like lone wolves". *Green Boat* is a picture frozen in time and space and continues the poet's recurrence of themes like the past, the ghosts, the sea and open spaces.

The author also includes some Japanese Tanka poems. As in the haiku, or in the sonnet, it is important that the poet grasps and conveys thoughts and notions into the strict composition of these type of poems. Fenech achieves that marvelously in *Dawn* which is sweet and self-standing.

Waves is another Tanka, a thundering poem where he compares the open sail to "a brandished scimitar". *Jilted* is caustic and naturalistic, also revealing and didactic whilst *Innocence of Old* is dreamy. *Concrete Jungle* is nostalgic and transmits criticism to environmental issues. *Voyage into the Light* is a personal view of death, perhaps the poet's intimate longings as to how he wants to leave this world, which reminded me of Shakespeare's monologue in Hamlet: "To Be or Not to Be: to die, to sleep, no more". Same idea in both poets: the peaceful departure, the sense of quiet death.

There are many more poems which will make readers ponder more seriously about life in general. The poet seems determined to send direct messages in a well-crafted language, revealing his journalistic background in making every single word count.

Reading Ray's poems embarks readers on a voyage in time and space at roller-coaster speed. He is blessed

with his special gift of this compelling bulldozer style poetry, full of love and friendship, from his photographic memory that allows readers to peek into his past and tremble. It seems as if each reader will find himself reflected in these provocative, enticing lines, and is taken on a cleansing, redemption ride to their origins, fears or hopes.

1. Palabras de Pablo Neruda (Words by Pablo Neruda). Neruda 2004, pp. 34-35 (post mortem).
2. The quotations from Raymond Fenech are taken from his biography or his poems in the book I am reviewing, Nostalgia.
3. All the quotations by Shakespeare in this review were taken from Complete Works of William Shakespeare. Volume XIII, chiefly the Sonnet section, and also from the play Hamlet. David McKay Publisher (the year not available).
4. All the quotations of the poems taken from En el corazón de un poeta (In a Poet's Heart). Selection by Esteban Llorach Ramos. Cuban Book Institute. Publishing House of Special Editions. 2006. This quotation belongs to the poem El sexo (Sex) by Pablo Neruda (1960). All translations by the reviewer.
5. The Literature of the U.S.A. Publishing House People and Education. Cuba. 1983.
6. Palabras de Pablo Neruda (Words by Pablo Neruda). Neruda 2004, pp. 34-35 (post mortem)

About The Reviewer

MIGUEL ÁNGEL OLIVÉ IGLESIAS M.Sc.- Associate Professor of Holguín University, Cuba. Miguel Ángel Olivé Iglesias, M.Sc. is the Cuban Canada Cuba Literary Alliance (CCLA) President, member of the Mexican Association of Language and Literature Professors, and Vice-president of the William Shakespeare Studies Centre. Miguel Ángel Olivé Iglesias (1965), a.k.a. Michael, teaches English and is an Associate Professor, has a Bachelor's Degree in Education (Major in English), and a Master's Degree in Pedagogical Sciences. He has been teaching for thirty years, and writes poems and stories in Spanish and English. His work has been featured in numerous CCLA publications. His scientific writing on foreign language teaching, values education, interdisciplinary issues and other topics have been discussed in national and international forums, and published in Cuba, Spain, Canada and Mexico. He is currently involved in CCLA projects, and works at the Teacher Education English Department as a professor of English and English Stylistics and is also Head of the Discipline, Integrated English Practice.

Nostalgia & Time

Were they really here?

The sky was clear black,
The moon spilled its rays
Over the pebbled bay,
Waves splashed my feet:
Each time the cold sea
Woke me from my dreams.
Was it my salty tears
Running down my cheeks,
Or the sweat breaking
Into beaded bubbles
Trickling down my forehead?
This was just my fancy:
There was no moon
Nor rays, bay, or sea,
All had ebbed away
Frightened from decay.
Bluebottles buzzed noisily
On a decomposing starfish
Orange and bright red,
Rotting near dull fish
Killed by shiny blue oil slicks.
The houses from the past
Had lost their complexion,
Their architectural personality
Their glowing colours.
And from two-storey
Turned into high-rise buildings,
Dull concrete grey shadows
Prison cells for honest citizens:
A claustrophobic cluttering
That cloaked the gloaming star;
And when it rose again
The light couldn't penetrate

The gloomy veil on the streets.
The flowers on window sills
Were plastic made,
People's green fingers
Had been amputated.
All the trees and fields
The open spaces
Filled with fresh air;
The wilderness of winds
Cold winters and rains,
Summer's zephyr breath
That came and went
Had all been put to death.
Here lovers wooed,
Furtively whispering
Trivial sweet nothings
Into each other's ears,
Their faces rose-red
From their own tickling breath.
When they embraced
On hidden benches,
They carved their initials
To immortalize themselves
On carob tree branches.
These lovers, now ghosts
Of the past, have departed;
Their outline only painted
In moments and minutes,
Of fleeting reflections,
In vanished decades
In a blink of an eye;
When all their wishes
Burnt out with each falling star:
Whilst watching quiet seas,
When the sky was onyx black
And the moon spilled its rays

Like waves sploshing their foam
Over the white pebbled bay.
They knew then they were betrayed,
Their lives Time would finally claim
Nothing would be the same again
And nothing would remain.

Blinkers

He looked up at the sky with bleary eyes …
Through the darkness he saw no lights
Twinkling, same as when he was a child.
The blinkering was only in his mind and the pitch black
Felt like it was embracing his decrepit body.
It seemed like only yesterday when with his sister
He sat lying down on his back looking for satellites:
They distinguished them from stars standing still
As they moved fast across the open universe.
Then, they wondered if there were others like them
Observing earth as it turned slowly like a merry go-round;
Those nights had come and gone in split seconds.
His sister left home when he was seventeen,
From there on, he never looked at the night sky …
Nor to watch the long dark summer nights.
Those sky watchers left with their innocent childhood;
Never returned; there was nothing left to return to
The magic had all gone and with it his youth,
Those he loved and those he knew became one,
Now retained somewhere in his fading memory.
As he sat alone in the quiet of his room this winter,
Peered onto the empty pavement, the broken street lantern,
The moon was mirrored shinning in a fountain.
But even he was lonely, for the stars had been switched off.
The cold brought the day to a close without a sunset
The concrete buildings had cemented its face out forever:
Was it the Reaper that banged its scythe against the window
Or perhaps a ghost of some forgotten relative come to visit?
The warmth from the derelict house had turned weirdly icy,
His breath swirled from his nostrils into vacant spaces
With only the wind's whining for company - the open skies of old,
Those shiny blinkers no longer visible, voices deafeningly absent.

The Dream and the Glory

The ground upon which I walk
Is alien to me and the century I lived in
Too young with a different mentality.
I've paced this ground as if there was a mist
From my waist down and I couldn't see my feet,
Nor where each step fell and what lied beneath.
I've continuously thought I was in a nightmare,
That eventually it would all come to an end
With a sudden waking to a fanfare of reality;
My eyes would behold verity as I imagined it to be.
Only half of my spirit and body are here,
The rest of my being is beyond, aloof and alert,
In another time warp where innocence was bliss
And children still believed in fairy tales.

I've walked this earth thinking I could make a change
But I tripped over one delusion after another;
Human values and kindness wiped clear,
Love was all make belief, castles in the air;
Lovers came and went without any remorse
And I was left grieving out in the cold,
To contemplate where I had gone wrong;
Until I believed there was no heaven nor a God.
It was a time I realized 'the end' came all too often
And in real life no one lives happily ever after.
All I see reminds me of something that is gone
Into the abyss we try not to speak about:
Humans design their own dreams and glory
But when they succumb to the angel of death,
Where are their dreams, where is the glory?

Bridge into the Past
(Experimental Prose Poem)

I often come to this bridge. It's the most common thing to do at my age, when time seems to be escaping at tremendous pace. It's an invisible path that is only in my mind. When I think I'm losing touch with my past, with all the beautiful things I experienced, the people I loved, my incredible memories, I take a walk onto this bridge that leads me into a time warp. My sojourn there always seems to be very brief and most times when I return from the journey, I feel very sad. The voyage into my past often takes me to my childhood, when time seemed infinite and I was immortal. All the people I loved were there to stay and every ending had a fairy tale conclusion of, 'They Lived Happily Ever After'. Life was all about school, walks in the countryside, playing with friends, running in the open fields, watching sunsets, eating ice-creams and ice lollipops, swimming on sandy beaches and fishing on my small colourful boat. And when I wanted to feel even safer and elusive, I took shelter in my room guarded by many models of the Knights of Malta. It was right at the top of my house and the quiet seemed to join forces with the Knights that guarded it and kept it away from chaos. It's where I always wanted to be living my life – carefree, sheltered from evil witches and the bogeyman, with my family forever protected and safe. But in that life, there was also a bridge, which was a forbidden site. It was a place that none of us kids ever wanted to be near. But the day did come when I was forced to take the journey away from my safe haven and cross the bridge into reality. It was the hardest day of my life and it was my first day at work. I left the protective walls of my room, of my little world behind to venture into the dangerous world out-side, and which I knew very little about. Sheer courage

and determination kept me moving on into the unknown and for many years, I lost sight of the safe haven I had left behind. When I finally realized, it was too late, the bridge connecting the real world to my past had vanished, perhaps collapsed somewhere in the passage of time. The only way to find the bridge and cross it again was through the time warp, which I often managed to penetrate through my imaginative mind. The last time I visited, I walked for hours into a deserted place, where the poppy fields were replaced by concrete apartments and the colour of the sea was a rainbow of pollution. All the houses where my friends and family lived had been abandoned or demolished and all those I loved were gone forever.

The Swing in the Garden

The swing hangs creaking on the broken chain
screeching loudly in excruciating pain,
rusty, dribbling red blood and hanging lame
on winded years, day in day out the same.

How many a child has sat here and played,
how many on its wooden bucket swayed
before with age its outer skin was flayed?
Time flew, children grew; all to rest were laid.

Just memory of all those years remains
like photos shot in some special time frame,
sparked from an urge or mania to maintain
this life immortalize, or so we like to feign.

The swing hangs creaking on the broken chain
as summer breeze wistfully speaks in pain,
whispering about our joy and strain
like conscience when it pokes us hard in vain.

The swing squeals contemplating on the rain
joining chorus with time's tick-tocking refrain
of life that's been: will never be again,
while our dreams flee on a choo choo train.

The Silent City (Mdina)

To Charles Borg my Secondary School Literature Teacher

I found it all in the gateway
On the silent city slabs,
A silent tinge of solitude
That swept away the winds.

I could not but betray myself
To the lonely wisps of dawn,
For time I found to stop and think
About it more and more.

The pathless tunnel to the end
Of the human destiny,
Once one starts, one never stops
But goes on, on and on.

Note by the author: Mr. Borg was my literature teacher at St. Albert the Great College, from Form II to Form V. But he was not the same as other literature teachers - he was in love with all the poetry he taught me and an inspiration to my writing talent, which at that time had long been clearly defined. The above poem is one of the many I had showed him, asking for his opinion and advice. The very last line was edited to what you see above by this incredibly talented, but humble man, who was entirely dedicated to his students without ever even realizing how special he was. His enthusiasm was contagious and contributed in no small way to make me shift classes from sciences to arts and encouraging me to stay on course to become a poet and a writer. The next and last time I met Mr Borg was in unfortunate circumstances, when his house was burgled. At the time, I was working as a reporter for The Times of Malta and assigned to cover the burglary. Even under such circumstances, Mr Borg who was single welcomed me with great enthusiasm, especially because he realized I had followed his advice to pursue a writing career. The next time I heard about him was when I was told recently by an old school friend, he had sadly passed away. One thing I will never forget about that visit to his house was his study. It was exactly as I had imagined it to be, teeming with books and papers. But not only, he also told me his little secret and about a dream that never came into fruition: he was also a music composer. To this special mentor, my friend and inspiration, I want to express my gratitude for helping me through a rather bumpy road, and to achieve what was an impossible dream at that time. You are always in my heart and in my prayers. I will never forget you.

Tempus Fugit

How many mood sways
On this dull November day?
It's as if time has never been,
Nor my life, nor my kin;
Played fugitive, no sooner I was born
From the umbilical cord I was torn,
Became aware of life's forlorn hope
The continuous strife and strain,
Each day was like no other pain.

All Christmases were divine
So intertwined with family;
Days that warmed the heart,
The cold forced to stay outside.
Until one by one they all departed
And all their merriment was silenced:
When their lives were done,
Their souls were lost in the space of time
Congealed outside this mortal confine.

The only memories are in photos,
Dust-covered, each cobweb like a chain,
Incarcerating them on the other side
In some unknown spirit world;
And time, unlike when I was young
Now seems to drive a racing car:
Tempus, this immortal ghost *fugit*
Ruthless, with no sunset or dawn
Fast forward, it goes on, and on and on …

Roller Skating Down Memory Lane

If I could turn back the clock
I would roller skate at Rocky Vale
Before the new parish church was built,
And the road to Regional Road split the valley,
Broke the heart of the spring that trickled slowly
Upon pebbled stones turned green with moss.

I would go to hear the early morning Mass
At the 500-year old Our Lady of Conception Chapel,
As the fishermen's colourful *luzzi**
Berthed at the bay with their fresh daily catch.

I would go to gently pick caterpillars
From Spinola Palace Gardens' olive trees,
Admire their woolly green and yellow abdomen,
Preserve them in a glass-lidded jar
Until they turned into cabbage white butterflies.

Sit on the front porch in the summer night
And watch the star-studded skies;
Trying to distinguish stars from satellites.
Climb onto the roof garden to catch moths
Listen to crickets chirp and fiddle in the night
Stridulating a symphonic masterpiece.

Enjoy the cool fresh sea breeze,
Children's voices singing nursery rhymes
When 8 o'clock was curfew time,
When the world still believed in innocence;
People were mostly genuine, never put on an act;
Cars, designers' clothes and fashion were not important
As people's feelings, daily bread and sinless souls.

If I could turn back the clock,
If I could roller skate back in time
To this valley of innocence,
To a purely simplified and primitive life
Washed by rain water streams
Where I could wallow in the grass's mossy green.

Luzzi are traditional very colourful Maltese fishing boats

The Green Boat

Inside it my youth juggles with the ghosts
Frozen in the scent of weather-beaten wood.
Through its gaping crevices
I see the rust of the anchor
Bleeding around a fossilized starfish.
Seagulls make a cacophonic melody
As if teasing us humans for our limitations;
Proud of their natural potential
To fly, float and walk on land.
This time capsule of youth is shattered
By the gasman hooting his horn,
A weekly wakeup call for his customers.
Those summers are now like some forgotten tale
When fresh fish glittered in their armoured scales
And time hung on my fishing line,
Sinking into an abyss of green before it could age.
Wet fingers cut easily by nylon thread,
But no blood was ever drawn.

Ave Maria

Again I heard the great big bell
that floats on the evening's breeze,
the chime I've heard so often times
it lays my soul at peace;

For since a child I've listened to
this melancholic tune,
and each and every time I hear
it breaks my heart in two;

This gentle tinkle brings me grief
and echoes long and deep,
reminds me of all departed souls
for whom I pray and weep.

Feeding on Time

You haunt me so often
Like the wind on a wintry night,
Or the cruel sun that burns out
Every patch of the cool shade;
And I try hard to walk away
To run, escape from all the pain
You've been inflicting for years:
Leaving me deprived of joy.
And each time I hide from you,
The agony remains, I cannot shake
The ache you bring about each day.
A ghost invisible, you silently wait,
Then you leave and take with you
Part of my life, part of my youth,
Whilst I watch you turn from pink to grey
Till the light is defeated by darkness again.
Each day you syphon more energy;
At each sunset, I force myself to say:
Tomorrow, dawn will bring another day,
But then each thought for tomorrow
Is lost in the mist that blocks my way,
Through the pitch black, the dream
That turns into a wakeful nightmare.
Each corner I try to turn, I feel afraid
Not knowing what's on the other end;
But when I feel so vulnerably mortal
And everything dwells on such finality,
Deep down I know, I can only rely on today,
The madness of living, knowing I must die
Continue to feed on what's left of you, time.

Garden Café

Lemons haloed by clear blue
are surrounded by the madness of living,
an agitated melee of humans:
each face tells its own story, life
is slowly syphoned no sooner it begins.

And no one lives hundreds of years,
like this giant cypress tree.
Flies sip the remains from empty cups
of dark coffee or milked tea,
some lipstick-stained.

Time rewards us with momentary joy
the pleasure of a meal or a drink,
falling in love, having sex, expectations.
But like slaves we work in a mill
pushing the giant clock's hand forward,
round and round until the end.

Chillness emanates from these stones
that have taught history for centuries.
Silent spirits swish past unnoticed
seeking the path to the light;
they speak, but no one listens.

Growing With the Shadows

It took giant steps from that spring,
when the waddling child,
like a rubbery doll screamed in excitement,
tongue wagging inane language.
At times he seemed surprised,
and halted to listen to his own voice
emitting sounds like the many that came
from cages in the zoo.

His skin was like an armour seemingly
immune to summer's heat or cold:
he was unafraid even of Winter's dark shadows,
when old witches were tied to wheelchairs,
under a curse following confrontation
with the fairy godmother's magic wand.
And angels' wings were in his feet,
at the sight of a gap-toothed mouth
grinning evil in a wrinkled face.

The teacher's shadow on his desk,
her powdered face with red lips
he'd have liked to kiss as she towered
against a dark blue sky;
she sat on her chair, legs slightly apart,
white laced panties and suspenders showing.

The fall came with tramps
lighting bonfires to bake chestnuts;
an aroma of burning wood
that teased his hunger;
the coal-like lava burnt in cauldrons,
emanating an aura of red and orange sparks,
announcing Halloween and Christmas.

43

The green colour of fields
became brown, then tinted white,
many times, over and over again,
until the scenery existed only in a camera.
The bulldozers and cranes came
to abolish the fir trees and plushy fields,
to build concrete blocks of apartments
tasteless, long, grey shadow-makers
that seemed to have grown from marbled roots.

The days of the bogyman were over
the house of the cruel witch lay in ruins –
soon to be bulldozed into oblivion,
even though the child now grown
realized there was no evil there.
The only signs of the fall
were in the flower shops,
littered with dry decapitated leaves.

All Souls' Day

The orange colour of the fall
Is in every human's quickened pace
As darkness eats up the light
And shortened days dissipate
Into a huge empty space.
And Seagulls spin their yarn
About the old forgotten times,
When fishermen set down their sails
Before unloading their night's catch.

How my mood sways
On this dull November day,
It's as if time has never been
Nor my life, nor that of my kin;
Played fugitive, no sooner I was born
From the umbilical cord I was torn,
Became aware of life's forlorn hope,
Each dawn, each day was like no other pain.

All Christmases I recall were joyful
With family who came to dine;
Days that warmed the heart,
The cold was forced to stay outside.
Time flew in a blink of an eye
Before they all passed away:
Their laughter, their voices silenced
Their stories, mischief, misdemeanors
Now forgotten and laid eternally to rest,
Deep frozen in a frightening quiet place.

Photo albums are the only memories left,
Dust covered, each cobweb like a chain
Incarcerating them on the other side,
In some unknown spirit world;
And time, unlike when I was young
Now seems to drive a racing car:
Time, this accursed serial killer, escapes
Indestructible, immune to death,
Ticks inside our hearts like a ceaseless drum.
And before we know it our time is come.

The Hill and Karmena, the Egg Seller

I was here as a child dreaming about adulthood saying:
If only I was a grown-up, I would be free to steal
all happiness from the magic cauldron of life.
Forget about having to eat boiled eggs,
or having cod liver oil forced down my throat.
Life then was played forward and backwards
on chalk-drawn boxes on a pavement
where we seemed to balance our fortunes.
The rocks of the valley have been hewn away
by caterpillars that do not turn into butterflies.
*Karmena** breathes asthmatically up the tarmac hill
into fuming mists, tainting the whiteness of her fresh eggs.
In the old days I used to wait like a Leopard
ready to pounce as she approached within range:
to throw the balloon full of coloured water;
it flew high in the air dropping only few inches away from her.
Shocked she would shriek, tilting the basket full of eggs.
Then it seemed like the whole universe rolled down hill
onto plush green grass still wet with the squelching dew.
Since then, birds have lost their nests in the trees
and people are forced to live in concrete-like prisons.
Karmena died and her farm turned into apartments.
House keys can no longer be left in the locks,
hearts have hardened, so Valentine comes only on the 14th
and material things are all that have significance.
Time ebbs furtively away as if it doesn't want to hurt us
leaving only memories hanging like portraits,
and empty cauldrons with no magic or joy to steal from.

*Karmena is the name, Carmen in Maltese. She used to come regularly to our house to sell my mother fresh eggs from her farm situated in one of the old narrow streets of St. Julian, once full of beautiful houses of character, most of which all had massive gardens. The majority of these houses, including Carmen's farm have been replaced by hideous concrete apartments because the local

governments we have had in the last 35 years have given the green light to all the building contractors to build whatever they want, wherever they want, even if these senseless, tasteless, minute, overpriced apartments have taken away the privacy and the natural sunlight from the remaining old houses, creating serious parking problems and a claustrophobic environment. The reason for this is simple. Every politician running for the general elections is largely sponsored by the same building contractors and other businessmen. So basically, the country is being run by businessmen and John Citizens have no say in all this, even if there is a governmental organization called, the Malta Environment Planning Authority that is supposed to protect and conserve old buildings, as well as protect the rights of citizens from the hassles and all the inconveniences created by the building contractors. Unfortunately, these are backed by local politicians and have become untouchable. Building contractors in Malta are the most powerful people and can literally, no pun intended, bulldoze their way roughshod over anyone and everything.

Shadows Never Grow Less

Voices ring in perpetual motion
with the wind - faces in spaces,
old and young, timid and bold.
Centuries ate off chunks from these walls.
The sea lashes at slippery pebbles,
shiny ingots, that light the green moss.

This house has seen decades of
babies born, men enter these walls.
Many hung up their hats, wiped their boots,
on tartan mats, laid down their walking sticks
to join in a Christmas or anniversary party;
when the aphrodisiac smell of oven-baked rice
with happiness lit up their jolly faces.

Making people jovial those days was easy:
they came from all walks of life,
from simple laymen, priests to ministers.
Together they clinked champagne glasses
and drank to a long healthy life saying:
May your shadow never grow less!

The festive sounds have long faded in time
like the wooden cots with dolls and teddy bears,
and dust has seeped through the window cracks
laying layer upon layer, burying those centuries past.
Since then, many stars have fallen and burned out
and the years have sought refuge in crevices,
like the many skin-coloured lizards time has shriveled.

Summer Place

If I were to be asked:
What is your greatest wish?
I would simply answer:
To be reborn in the 50s!
When not far from my home
Was the sea
Spread open fields
Brown and green;
Idyllic views
Rich with nature's scents
And freshly caught fish,
Armoured in silver scales
Spread on sea lettuce
In yellow wicker baskets.
And when the ascending sun
Turned the sky rosy pink,
The breeze twiddled my hair
With invisible fingers
Seemed to tease,
Inviting me to play
With an imaginary friend.
And my future princess
Whom I still hadn't met,
Only her outline was visible
In the lazy summery wake.
On the other side,
Open meadows were coloured
By poppies like gaping lips
Deep red, purple or pink,
As if conversing with the wind;
Coloured rainbows arched
Across a clear horizon
As far as the eye could see,

Where each evening the sun
Nestled in between the hills;
Each time it winked at me
With its last gentle rays:
Tranquillity reigned supreme,
And far, far away church bells pealed
Tinkling on the breeze, the *Ave Maria*.
While the farm dogs
Greeted their master
As he returned home
From his nearby fields.

If only I could join
These ghostly spirits,
Enjoy that feeling of safety
When principles and values
Were more important than wealth;
When people were humans
And nothing else mattered.
Families lived on one salary
And children could always count
On their mothers' presence
From birth to teenage:
Whenever they needed to cry,
Each time they thought
It was the end of the world;
Each time they collapsed
Their parents were there
With rosary beads in hand,
Together knelt down
To recite the rosary,
Knowing the Lord would intervene.
As a child, countless times
When afflicted by fever
My parents slept by my side.

Often I woke up screaming
From terrible nightmares,
About evil shadows from life's reality.
Comforted by their soothing voices
That hushed my relentless sobbing,
Their hands gently wiped away my tears
Singing me a sweet lullaby;
Until I drifted into deep sleep
Dreamed about the magic Fairy Queen,
The knight in shining armour protecting me,
My Guardian Angel, now I can no longer see.

The Primary School Classroom (1965)

Lightning flashed. All pupils were whipped awake.
Shiny arrows flew across the sky thick like candy floss.
The voice was smothered in dumbstruck stillness.
The teacher was no superman. He was frightened and cross.

The Alps closed in. Hannibal marched on plastered walls.
Death, blood red, drowned in spoils of Roman wars.
Among the prize winning watercolour paintings was mine.
Depicting a gory battle, where soldiers fight until they fall.

Tempus fugit. The old carob tree was like a hunchback.
It whispered something I couldn't catch, from the past.
I listened hard, but the breeze blew in gale force winds.
And the tune changed from rock to rap and talking fast.

Years are fossilized like roots grappling with death.
I travelled, bought souvenirs to remind me of mystery:
Since I was born, men have been to the moon and back.
Suddenly it's the year 2000: the present becomes history.

The Christmas Spirit of Old
(To my parents who gave me so many of these Christmases)

Christmas is always a feast that wakes the human senses
brings to life all extra sensory perception,
when memories rally our hearts, time becomes insignificant.

I pledged all my childhood to this feast of colour and lights,
aromatic oven-baked macaroni, chestnuts cooked in caldrons
when Christmas ghosts floated from the warm fierce flames.

The sizzling fried date slices filled the air with fragrant flavours
of brandy and Anise and many other festive sweet delights;
the pine tree branches were lit with minute-like fire fly lights.

Imaginative fairies with their flaming wings shed glittering sparks,
that flitted fresh flamboyantly from their golden magic wands.
The Holy Night was personified in humble home-made cribs;

made of thick brown paper, or rustic stone and sand,
populated with clay figurines of heroes that lived their lives to the full,
like us struggled against those who abused the weak and glorified evil.

This was a time for family to rejoice singing Christmas carols,
and many accompanied the procession of the newly born Baby Jesus
when lanterns flooded darkness and wealth was measured by the spirit.

Even love, in those days was platonic, romantic, harmonic.
It signified true family values, took us ages to learn its true significance
but finally it was there to stay, until childhood formed wrinkles with age,
the young couple grew grey but even then dementia was powerless
and even after they passed, it could not take their immortal love away.

The Dorian Gray Shock

Every single thought
That haunts my mind
Takes me back in time
To all those people
I loved, some still here,
Some have passed,
Some many moons ago;
And though they're gone
They are still here,
In my heart, in my soul,
In memories of long ago.
Each one of them
Shared with me his wisdom:
To stay human, expect pain,
To endure it, even when
This feels impossibly insane;
To move on, to fight, survive,
Think only of values
That really count,
The reason I was born
The reason I must die.
Whether it's the Fall
When their voices screech
Through fissured walls,
Or whisper in my ears
On a breeze in spring,
Or deafen me in winter
With their hallowed howls,
I still listen to their stories.
I've learnt with age
When I was born
Time slips out of its cage
Furtive, like a silent thief.

The clock is its beating heart:
At first, it walks at snail's pace,
Deludes me it will never pass
And I will never grow,
That childhood is immortal,
I would remain a child forever
Eternal, immune to death;
It's what it made me believe.
Now I look at the mirror
After all this time and know
I have been mocked:
And I am still to recover
From the Dorian Gray's shock.

The Picture

A weeping willow
bends under its own weight
besides a discoloured lake,
from a picture yellow with age,
a scene pivoting on time.

In it is my dream garden,
what my mother looked at
when washing the plates;
while every fugitive day passed
with ever increasing pace.

Often my mind would imagine:
*What if I could float right through
the window picture, walk into my dream,
integrate myself with its silent wisdom
live on that side maybe for a while?*

When my childhood home was sold
the window picture was left behind.
My only wish is to go back in time,
to the weeping willow by the lake
left there with the house to be torn apart.

Gladiolus
(To my father who loved Sword Lilies)

They have grown unfailingly each year
for many years since your green fingers
planted the bloodless bulbs,
that grow pink like the inside of a vagina.
Too many years to remember
too many events you were part of.
Smiling through your pain,
the contortions of your mouth
were even more terrifying
on your handsome face.
The Sword Lilies you sowed
seem like you're re-visiting
each time they grow.
Now every spring I wait for them to bloom
to see your face again in them pain-free.
Perhaps a few more springs will pass,
and when they fail to grow,
I'll know you're calling me.

My Great Aunt's House at Zejtun

My soul melted in the walls
and half of me had died,
like the well's gelid stones
in the courtyard when night falls.

Low arches touched my head,
each time I bowed, it seemed
in reverence to centuries
born on this four poster bed.

History spoke from picture frames,
when men wore bowler hats;
scowled deep through waxed moustache,
long gone in sixty decades.

Like film star macho men
with hats tilted on one side,
a cigarette between the fingers
as if the world belonged to them.

When the last key locked the door
memories screamed inside,
children's laughter died in silence,
ghostly footprints marked the floor.

The Last Appassionata to My Mother

Beethoven's Appassionata reverberated
sweeping from wall to wall,
as I stood silent in the hall,
she'll never play it any more.

Scores lay where she'd last played
with gusto, love and pain
when her arthritic fingers
touched down heavy on every note,
like an uncontrollable weight.

Recalled how her frail figure would emerge
smiling in the sun-filled corridor,
as I knocked gently on the glass door,
almost afraid of smoldering the tune,
this scene was a *déjà vu.*

Outside, a cacophony of sounds
far from Beethoven, Mozart or Bach,
a pollution of noise drowned the past,
all that was noble of value that lasts.

Those early summer mornings
when *Ix-Xejka** limped up the porch
fresh *sargu** in hand; dog waiting on the stairs,
as he wrapped the fish in newspapers,
then hobbled away to our next door neighbour.

The house stood strong for decades and more
its walls like a fortress now thick with moss;
crevices empty of crickets that chirped,
when the summer night crept gently from light
and mama's fingers sung us a lullaby.

Beethoven's Appassionata reverberated
through these double built walls,
my refuge for decades from spring to the fall:
now this last melody as the curtains are drawn.

*Ix-Xejka nickname of an old fisherman, Karmnu (Charles)
*Sargu (Sunbeam)

A Grain of Sand

I am like a single grain
of sand in a desert -

blown about by winds
onto several pathways

effecting people's lives
in miniature proportions

threatening to blind
when angered

or serving as a soft warm
bed on a sunny beach

the wind is my friend
the sun fires my soul

I am men's worse enemy
when I am used to measure time

I am golden like a star
without a shine -

this grain does not feel pain
to think that all worldly pain

is buried beneath this grain
of sand in the desert.

The Fortified Bedroom

In the hours of sleep, bed was the safest place on earth
where childhood dreams stole me away to wander and flirt
with guardian angels, who kept me safe from places where danger lurks.

On the shelves, the armoured knights with spears and bastard swords
looked down ready to charge on their steeds with a battling roar
against any ghoul or dragon who would dare in my direction soar.

Childhood's innocence was then protected by cleansing seas
that swept evil shadows away as they lay ready to pounce on me,
hiding inside cauldrons full of stagnant brew under the witch's tree.

Magic broke curses cast by ghouls, slipped beneath my bedroom door
as waves of endless blue lapped against the shingled shore,
kept me safe and sound, far away from all the painful worldly gore.

From long ago I still can hear elven fairies whisper gently in my ears
as their soft spoken words tickled my hair: *There is nothing to fear
for fancy will always light the way, from danger keep you clear.*

But even then, I could hear the screaming beyond these walls
of people who had no vivid dreams to keep them warm at all,
but as I grew, I was forced to join them and their despairing calls.

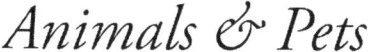

Animals & Pets

An Apology to Pooch
(1999-2011)

Your 19-inch collar weighed in my hands
like it had never weighed before,
still warm with your name inscribed on the medallion.
I placed it in a box and hid it in the attic.
Perhaps I put you through unnecessary pain,
should never have allowed the operation,
the seven inch cut in your belly
that caused you excruciating pain,
contorting your brown blind eyes
that never lost their loving gaze,
not even for a moment.
I want to apologise my friend
for the pain I caused you towards the end,
when you were in agony and I was angry;
when the K9 immune treats were withheld by customs,
the only hope for your salvation.
I want to apologise for my inability to put up a fight,
not using enough force to give you your last chance.
When your cancer took away your huge appetite
and you kept turning your head away, even from fried liver
my anger increased - I was losing the battle.
I want to apologise for being weak
when I should have been strong,
for having put you to sleep, you my best friend,
who was crucial in my fight against cancer.
I repaid you by allowing the vet
to pierce your heart with poison.
Yet you placed your head in my hand,
your last gesture, as if I was your saviour;
your unconditional love, your faith in me to the very end relentless.
It was as if you were whispering to me:

Please let me go - it's time - don't worry.
You crossed Rainbow Bridge without me.
When I look back, I cannot come to terms with your departure,
wish my breathing was controlled by a switch
so I could turn it off to take away the pain.
I apologise my friend for being such a coward.

Death of a Stray Cat

It moves slowly squatting on its hind legs
Eyes glimmering yellow agony;
This is the last
Of its nine lives already spent.
The cold spits its anger in convulsive rage.
Like crystal bullets the hail
Unloads pelting its rib cage.
Its last meow sounds
Like a new born child.
Smoke from chimneys bursts
Forming breath-like clouds,
Vanishes into frozen lights.

It searches for shelter,
Shakes gelid water from its paws.
It wishfully eyes the high wall,
But its swift perfect agility
Is only in the distant past.
Darkness closes in,
The rain drizzles to a stop.
There is no sound or stir.
The milk in the plate remains untouched.

In Memoriam: To Rex I
(1972 - 1985)

A dog barked in the distance,
broke sunset into glimmering shards,
of burning sparklers on liquid glass.
Rex sat on the fortress's wall
a silhouetted outline of lion's mane;
his head on one side, ears cocked
listening to everything I couldn't hear …

The last trip in my car:
his huge front paws hung motionless.
We carried him inside the room,
with the pungent odour of surgical spirit;
his dry nose caught the whiff:
at his best he would have wrenched my arm off
to get away from this ...

I felt as if I had betrayed him:
with one reassuring hand
I patted the dull brown colour
of his sagging massive coat,
until the vet sank the needle
into his fast beating heart.

His last glance at me was different,
between faithful and diffident:
I've seen it ever since
in every sunset at the old fortress.

The Old Retriever

It limps across the street
dragging its right hind leg
staggering beneath its weight.
Cars dash by dangerously close
to non-existent destinations
chasing their beaming headlamps,
away in an instant flash.

Sunset reflects
people's doubles
as they cross the street;
a bit like visible ghosts -
ahead or behind,
tall or incredibly fat,
to the right to the left,
fleeting across,
or standing faceless on the wall.

The dog waits at the gate,
barks hoarsely, once, twice,
until it slowly opens.
It wags its tail, limps inside,
leaving the scuttling shadows behind.

Human Strife

Hereafter

If only the misery and sorrow that surround me
Were not reflected in my own eyes,
Then I would see more clearly through the haze,
The mists, the clouds that fold and unfold
Before every step I take unto this long road.

If only my vision was blurred and was totally blind
Immune to humans crying tears of blood,
And somehow that magic wand I always longed for,
Since I was a child came into my hands,
So I could make things better, remove the pain forever.

If only my late loved ones could continue to speak
To communicate, to advise me, still feel their love
The comforting touch of their hands, feel their warmth;
And each time I close my eyes, I see their smile
Know for sure they're better off where they are.

If only when the sun sets, the rosy pink turns black
When my mind is devoured by memories that bring back,
The joy and grief I had: only then my parents were there
To cancel forever my fear, wipe away my tears;
To sing me a lullaby, kneel down with me to say a prayer.

If only I could go back and speak to those
I never said, *I love you*, for pride or momentary anger,
And they departed and I was left to say I'm sorry
Without ever knowing whether I had been forgiven:
Now anguished I strive on existing, instead of living.

If only I could watch a virgin world when rains were pure
And spoke with shades that spoke right back to me,
Strolled among nature's wilderness, when dew caressed my knees,
When yellow carpets in the fields swayed dancing in the winds
The sea was emerald blue like in a blissful fairy dream.

If only I could go back and be born already a man
Instead of a child, with the wisdom of a grown-up;
And knew already about life, the time that makes it tick,
So when death strikes I would not even know, or be afraid
Never miss my loved ones, and quietly sleep until I simply fade.

My Last Battle

It came straight without a warning
From an amber red sky,
When black clouds gathered
Like sinister fog gathers
In a Nosferatu gothic novel,
Creeping with freezing cold fingers;
Then it lit the sky with lightening
Frightening away the silent night.
I was not afraid of the beautiful storm
It came rapidly to dismantle my spirit,
But I looked it in the eye fearlessly
Shocked by courage it went into remission.
And I was still here to watch the calm
After the devastation, the fallen
Knights of my childhood
Had descended bravely to face it,
Waving their bastard swords,
Swinging them from left to right
Right to left holding their shields
In an impenetrable battle formation,
Protecting me, even as one by one
They fell under its sweeping wrath,
In all its urgency to kill me.
The water turned to blood.
The sea turned sour, the green weed
Washed ashore turned to piles of entrails.
Only half conscience I had fought alongside;
Now my dreams shattered,
Impossible to put together
Dreams that had given me so much joy
Whilst grief was left behind, but only for a while
Throughout this short journey of mine.

I was alive but I knew the end was closing in
And all would eventually come to naught;
But I did not despair because my spirit
Will always remain here,
Will never die, nor will it wither:
Instead, it will flourish into the immortal air;
The pain, the fear, grief and death
All shed away from my memory
No more, no more pining, painful breathing.
I will have one last sleep now
And it will be peacefully forever.

Rebellion

Throughout this journey I have been feeling the pain
But how strange, now I no longer complain,
Now it's turned into defiance, anger and rage
And my arms at times despite my thrombosed veins
Itch, the muscles strengthen into a wrestler's head-scissors
And I imagine my tormentors struggling helplessly
As I choke their life and breath out of them, but not completely;
For I release my hold only to resume the pressure as soon as they revive
So I can torment them, over and over until their necks are crushed.
And I stand over them; brush myself down, spit on their carcass.
But it would not be over until the angels from hell come
Crawl from beneath the ground, watch them gnaw their entrails
To drag them into their torture chamber, Dante's Inferno.
And with my forked spear I follow to continue what I started:
Among the flames, I will incise my name on their flesh to tell God:
Look where my kindness has got me; were you there to see
This evil submerge my life in grief despite all my kindness?
Have you forgotten me, have you forgotten I am also human
With a heart that once dwelt on mercifulness and charity?
Now, now, I'm the devil's advocate and have come to realize
Humans are bad, their evil stems from the pits of their bellies:
They did not come from the Garden of Eden but straight from hell. When
I called you, you shunned me away, you ignored my tears
The abundance of my benevolence; the angels' wings I wore
That I had to shed using a sword of fire and the joy turned sour.
As I stood looking over my past, I saw nothing but debris,
The debris of my life, the broken bits and pieces I left behind
All the good people you took away without blinking an eye;
My prayers for mercy, for a little reprieve left hanging out to dry.
I was not one of your angels, with that I agree but I acted like one
And each time I helped my fellow men, drank from their fountain of grief,
Stood by them through thick and thin, no matter their forlorn state

Yet still, you turned your face away and left, shrugging your shoulders
When you could have stayed, or at least taken me with you away.
From childhood, you knew I was not made strong or cold blooded enough
To live in this vale of tears; you saw I was aching all over, body and mind,
Each time I saw what this cruel world had to offer to the good people.
When my dog, though blind felt the Reaper closing in on me he bayed:
He felt its sinister presence, locked his fangs into its long sinewy arms.
The reaper ran and you left me here again to continue with the struggle,
To help others I didn't even know, who then turned their back upon me.
To you I say, if you are truly a merciful God, take heed for when this body
Its tired heart stops beating, this frame disintegrates, I will seek you out
Demanding full explanations: what harm did I do not to deserve reprieve?

Everything = Nothing
(A Double Dictum)

Nothing is everything
and everything is nothing;
if you have everything
you have nothing
because everything
for humans is based
on an expiry date
we all have it inscribed
within us in invisible ink:
so everything = nothing.

As long as we die
and death turns
everything into nothing,
when the spirit rises
nothing becomes everything.

Then we can see again:
our humane blindness
collapses like a veil,
it's when the real light
will enlighten our minds.

Finally, we will understand
the purpose of this journey,
why the everything
really meant nothing:
the human misconception
of having everything,
and nothing are indivisible.

We move on into time
to live and then die;
through our eyes
tight shut it's like
we've never been,
like we've never thought
never laughed, or cried,
and all the joy, grief
counted for nothing.

The immense pain,
a thousand moments,
memories come back in flashes,
captured photos in a camera
of people we loved;
some had everything
others had nothing.

Yet all passed away
like dust and sand,
into what we call time,
nothing and everything
remains in an open space
merely ghosts whispering.

Our hearts defy the odds
still beat on like drums,
until the rhythm
gets slower with every
sunset and every sunrise.

Nothing is everything
and everything is nothing;
if you have everything
you have nothing
because everything
for humans is based
on an expiry date
we all have it inscribed
within us in invisible ink:
so everything = nothing.

This Will Never happen to me Syndrome

There is Christmas, Easter and Valentine but also depressing advertisements about cancer. Outside - the slime and sleet - endless winter. Never before had I seen all this from the current perspective. Yet, I'm weighted down moving forward, backwards, dropping on my knees struggling to my feet, trying to stay up, only to be knocked down again. It all started when I began losing weight. I tried to emulate my hero Rocky Balboa, his joy of living, winning against all odds. But how can one train to fight cancer? I wanted to wake up people who worry about trivialities make them realize health is never a sacrosanct right. But they all suffer from the, *This will never happen to me syndrome!*

Hodgkin's Lymphoma and a stroke broke me down into shards, like a fallen porcelain moon. I thought I was safe on my way to a new red summer dawn - could already feel the warmth. I was derailed, impaled by the sword of fate. Now, I stand again, shrug off the pain trying to regain, to cease, to feign, change a sorrowful sunset, into a happy refrain. My heart sinks at every passing day, be it summer, the fall, winter or spring. When it's freezing, I grit my teeth, uplift my frightened heart and try to smoulder its weakened beat.

The day dawns with difficulty to breathe, gelid cold, incontrollable shakes and profuse sweating, the endless rest in hospital. There are plastic flowers in the vase, which I envy for their immortality - the stench of surgical spirit. Fourteen hours of painful chemotherapy: dripping orange liquid and a torturous injection that lasts five minutes. I am forced to listen to my heart beat, stare at the blood stain on the carpet from my punctured arm whilst doctors try to find a non-thrombosed vein …

Should I immerse myself into a sob story no one wants to hear, start over standing tall, even if I fall, wait for another dawn? Time has clipped Pegasus's wings, his unicorn trimmed. So I will call out my fearsome 300 Spartans to turn this scuffle into a last spectacular tussle.

To Sadness

Sadness what are you?
Where do you come from?
How do you dominate my heart?
Your breath I feel cold and gelid
As you caress my forehead.
Indifferent to all seasons,
You steal softly, silently
Through sunset breezes.
You seem to know when to slither
In between dark shadows
Like a spectre invisible,
To ambush and wreak havoc
In the gentlest way, ooze past
Any barrier, any fortress;
So when your elixir I breathe in
I hardly ever notice you are within:
Until wistfulness moves in
To rekindle my memories:
Mostly happy ones of childhood, youth,
Love and people who are no longer here.
When you sadness ambush my mind,
Your bitter sweetness always lasts a while
Before I know you have taken over my soul;
My mind you leave in disarray,
I know not what you are to this day,
Where you come from
And how you dominate my heart.

The Bird of Paradise
(To Angela)

The single Bird of Paradise was placed in a vase
Life and beauty embedded in a rainbow
That lit up the gloom in the room.
In September, the flower had bloomed
In the front garden of our new home
While I lay in hospital dying of cancer.
If only we exist briefly but magnificently,
Without pain, strife, always wanting more
It matters how we live, not how we die.

Moments of happiness, love and glory
Are in its fan-like crown of evergreen foliage.
And even though it knows it must die
It never feels pain, anguish or fear.
The green, red, purple and bright orange
Were also in my childhood's paint box:
My elixir of joy, invulnerability, immortality,
An immunity from my worst nightmares.
For childhood in our minds seems eternal
Steams ahead at full speed forever after,
So, we are deluded to think, until reality rushes in.

From a fleeting glance this flower stands regal
Defying the odds, indifferent even to death:
Unlike my body, a cadaverous map of veins,
Yet it shouts to all: We must live life to the full!
My bruised hands are punctured by needles,
The night is unfazed by my agony;
If only I could switch off this relentless pain.
Time and again, the flower's head plumage
Will explode kaleidoscopic and spectral,
Like human glory – the ever deluding myth.

The Waiting Room

In the waiting room made of lime stone
the lawyers are blank faces.
No colours, black, chequered suits, white ties
like the ghosts haunting this house.

Time screeches away the centuries,
the wind calls through fissured walls.
Time drags the clock's pendulum into a tick tock;
icy draughts seep through rock hard chairs.

The cold in the justice meted out
snaps sharply from a photocopier,
letter after letter, in clicking sequence
to match boring skies polluted with diesel.

The secretary's pink tight blouse
matches the tight slacks hugging her curves,
as she moves to a Brazilian rhythm,
glancing to see if she is being admired.

She sits crossing her legs her ample flanks
filling the chair, her jellified assets
spilling over her computer, knowledge undisputed
whilst conducting her boss's warfare.

Silence is only broken by the occasional
electric doors swishing open or shut,
like the curtains on a stage
of so many incredible life sagas.

People sleep nodding in the long wait,
their chins slammed into their chests.
Endless files stand like tomb stones
futile efforts that must all come to an end.

The Glory and the Strife

Do not leave this world
Thinking you have conquered it,
This earthly voyage is deceiving
Every past joy turns to grieving.
You might reach out for the moon
But the white melts from its face
Like burning wax from a candle,
Drops on shards of glittering waves
Where the night feeds on our fears,
We survive on hopes that are unclear.
The days of innocence are gone
Wrestled away from our childish sphere
The old rusty swing is bleeding tears
From forgotten days brimming with cheer.

Our lives are full of illusions
A story teller flicking through pages;
Takes you on a long tough test
Whether for real or in your fancy fest,
When your inner sight ceases to gleam
When your quest becomes extreme.
You stop, glance at the mirror,
You are not there, you're in a trance,
Like a furtive ghost, life passes
An electric storm, invisible gasses:
Are you really there as time bypasses
All that your memory compasses?
Are we really here, did we live this life,
Or is all forgotten, the glory and the strife?

A Sonnet with some Advice
(Shakespearian sonnet)

In troubled times consider just one thing:
That we're only here on a short-term stay,
That life passes us by in just a wink;
Love and passion extinguish like a flame.

When dreams and folly no longer pulsate
When the heart beat slows to a breath-like breeze,
We glance at the mirror watching men's fate,
As we count the last foliage on the trees.

Now what has been done cannot be undone,
We must go back to our childhood dreams
To all those things imagined just for fun,
Before future becomes what could have been.

If you have health, there's nothing more you need,
Except your smile and let God take the lead.

The Angel

The angel
Kneels down
With hollow sight
Staring into space,
Wings spread
Praying for the dead.
Each tomb ahead
Has an epitaph
Sculpted, some illegible.
Moss covers
Its reverent eyes
Looking as they sleep;
Whilst humans weep.

The sun moves,
It spreads its wings,
Then closes them again
In a silent flutter:
And we hope
Our loved ones
Are not there,
But in a spirit world;
Not in the cold
Confined space,
But in a quiet place
Where no harm
Can come to them.

First Blood

Plants don't get cancer – we do
mine came like a lightning bolt
split the darkness of self-assurance
and left my soul in crystal shards.

The first blood is drawn with the injection of burning chemo

As I look at the white walls around
there are bloodstains full of human effort
each drop tells its own story of too many
white or too little red cells.

Eventually it will burn my spirit and my hair will fall out

I could read it in their faces:
"this cannot happen to me",
just like I used to think before it happened
but it will cure after I've died a dozen times.

The chemo comes in lollipop orange colour and transparent gin

Every drip is an ocean
like a drop of TNT that travels
through the sea of blue on the wall
into mapped veins and blurred vision.

Hearing your heart beat for 144 hours of drip

Just as the light diminishes
the leaves of the flowered curtains turn grey
into a nauseating smell of aftershave -
as the nurse walks in to check my pulse.

The last remaining strength is killed, the price for more sunsets

Two doctors discuss the Da Vinci Code
the room is wiser but I prefer Harry Potter
with each passing hour this elixir
of life kills more hair follicles.

The sun seems so far away – All Souls' Day is in church bells

I am not who I was before this day
but what I will be tomorrow
after the long sleepless night
and forgotten dreams of Captain Nemo.

Only now I notice the preciousness of the dark outside.

Forgotten Fairy-Tales

His first orgasm took his innocence away …
All bed time stories –
Escaped from his sleep,
Soft like the feathers in his pillows,
Or the invisible clothes worn by the naked king.

The woman wore shorts under her skirt
Before she plunged down from the city entrance …
And he must have forgotten how Alice looked
When she slipped down the rabbit's hole
Into the dream world from which there was no exit.

He fell in love with his neighbour's wife …
Then came King Arthur
Who tripped on Excalibur
Betrayed by Guinevere and Sir Lancelot:
The sword sank with chivalry ages ago in the river.

His first love was his cousin …
He had forgotten all about Greek myths,
The flying unicorn, Pegasus
On which he had flown through many stormy nights,
When grown-ups feasted and parties were censored
And after 7p.m. was curfew time.

Erotic fantasy was soaking wet …
Childhood dreams were now vague
And children no longer believed
In Santa who was framed with rape:
Or Dickens' three ghosts of Christmas.

My Great Uncle's Funeral

Memories left a trail of debris
like a shower of soap bubbles bursting
from the ring of a wand dipped inside
a bottle, each globule a time capsule
of every human journey.
I remember the first person
peering down into my face,
gently poking my chin
with his rugged index finger.
My great uncle's loving smile,
my first giggle before a deluge of tears
grief, pain, then bereavement.
At his funeral, I was still seven.
We waited near an open grave.
It was the first I had ever seen.
Inside was so dark, I couldn't see the bottom.
The gloom was pitch black deep.
The freshly dug-up soil smelt musty.
My American cousins were dressed in pink.
The village band accompanied the coffin.
A fellow bandsman of my uncle led his peers
painfully limping in slow march,
holding the clarinet on a velvet cushion
with his band cap and its shiny badge.
My memory flashed back to his smiling face
as often times I puffed hideous sounds
from this same instrument
whilst he tried teaching me to play.
I couldn't understand the pain inside,
nor that I wouldn't see him again.
My parents said something about:
You'll meet him in heaven one day.

The way my father held on to my shoulders
seemed to me this was our last goodbye:
the pressure of his shaking hands
sent frightful tremors through my body.
I knew then adults were vulnerable too;
their dreams like mine bound to disintegrate
like the rainbow coloured soap bubbles
bursting in the air, leaving empty space.
Until then, I had the immortal sensation of youth
the misconception death would never prevail,
the illusion of each fairy tale I read:
And they lived happily ever after!

Operation – Traveling Towards the Light
(To my lovely wife, Angela)

Eyes travel ahead
like spotlights;
lasers fencing with darkness,
and the unknown.
On this cold metal bed
identity is on a plastic bracelet
and silence converses with itself.

I am no longer within
and the pain is gone.
For the first time
I am at peace
in a wakeful deep sleep.

Then a light appears through
closed lids,
blood-red like a ball of fire.
A sea in dreams
leaks through my eyes
staining the pillows.

Time freezes in my veins.
The Siberian cold chatters
with death until it leaves the room.
But only this time.

Life flows back
from the refrigerator
into red roses in the vase,
and the warmth of my wife's hand.

St. Mark's Elderly Home

Inside the room full of elderly
The sofa was like an island,
Abandoned as it had been soiled
Then dabbed with disinfectant.
You mustn't sit there, she whispered
 As if it were a top secret:
It's where Mary passed away in her sleep.

Mum was dozing in her wheel chair.
Her glasses slipping down her nose …
She stared blankly didn't recognize me:
I shouted in her ear, she caught my hand
Mumbled she was tired wanted to go to bed.
Her head drooped forward,
Rested on her skeletal chest.

Janet was being fed liquidised food:
She held the plastic cup and tried to drink
Her hands shaking - she couldn't lift it to her lips.
John was the only male, he was 102.
He often complained: *God has forgotten me*
here, when the only reprieve is death!

I walked towards my mother's room
To replenish her medicines,
Toothpaste that was never used.
Her telephone unplugged; she was blind and deaf;
In this past year she never phoned
Like she used to before sleeping every evening at 8.

I passed by Lydia's room, a prim and proper lady
who loved reading and music. The door was closed.
I asked the nurse if she was in - she pointed her finger:
Two small bags full of clothes were outside her room.
Lydia is gone, she is in hospital dying of cancer;
they pop off so suddenly so quickly:
they go to hospital and never come back.

I only realized today, life is a waiting game
Full of false expectations; we are mocked
That growing up, independence, the future,
Is a fairy-tale ending of happy everlasting life.
But this journey is brief, it's over in a blink of an eye
And before we know it, we are all waiting for God.

The Parting

Her Omega wrist-watch was still ticking
like her heart, only few hours before.
As I watched over the empty bed
I picked the handkerchief still wet
with her last fearful tears;
the bottle of *Anais Anais*
partially open as I had tried
to mask the smell of surgical spirit;
took the loop of silver hair I cut neatly
before her corpse was carried away.

Time grows very late, decades
of love, passion, jealousy and hate
were swallowed in a day.
I could almost hear her whispering,
repeatedly my father's name, *Vincent.*
She insisted he was in the room:
Smiling like a Cheshire cat.
To her, he had never passed away
her hero bearing the KOMR badge,
rifle slung on his shoulder,
smart in his khaki uniform:
*With the soppy look
in his enormous brown eyes.*
She was sixteen when she saw him the first time
never ceased to love him:
Bqajna ninhabbu sa l-ahhar nifs*,
were the last words on her dying lips.

*We loved each other until our last breath

The nightlights flickered like ghosts:
that Christmas she contracted pneumonia
on New Year's Eve she departed.
Back home, silence broke my eardrums
my heartbeat reverberated its tick tock,
more mileage on the clock in systematic rhythm;
with the loud chiming grandfather clock
standing against the creviced humid wall,
where the orange paint was crispy flaked.
Her laundry basket's lid sliding off the top
worn, empty, except for a pair of old socks.

What Ever Happened to Aunt Mary

The church bells chimed the *Ave Maria*
one of a thousand times;
breezes brought the melody
every evening at Aunt Mary,
a voice from a far distant past.

It started with the phone call at 7 a.m.
*Mary is being rushed to hospital,
she is feeling very ill.*
The call ended abruptly,
left me wondering in disbelief.

The house was tranquil;
when I entered her bedroom
the bed sheets were in a pile;
a fallen bottle on the commode
from which the acid had overflowed.

When my mother visited her,
she asked the all-important why?
*I heard when you drink acid
you immediately die,* she slurred
through swollen tongue and lips.

On 17th January 1979
my mother visited Aunt Mary
for the very last time.
She passed away that day
quietly into the wintry night.

The bells chimed the *Ave Maria*,
it was heartbreakingly sad;
the acrid stench of acid
from the bottle still lay by her bed,
indifferent to the life it had spent.

When Death Came to Visit

I was asleep or half awake
when death came to visit
creeping down the wall,
hollow eyes and hallowed face,
ready to swoop down,
with scythe ready to behead
those whose time on earth was done.
It searched carefully avoiding lights;
sunset was long gone and the light
was only in the warning red eye,
blinking on my chemo drip machine.
My thrombosed vein was blocked again
turning this into an endless night:
with each exhaling breath
life oozed out into the room
wreaking of surgical spirit;
the half deflated chemo bag
hung over my head
like a suspended sentence;
my weakness was in contrast
to the gale force winds outside.
I could only lay in fear
close my eyes, turn my face away:
each drop was a knife tearing into my vein.
The doctors came to search in vain,
each needle pinched my body numb,
blood flowed on the frosted sheets
from the eyes of Christ the Redeemer.

In Memoriam for My Father
(1920-1994)

The nurse asked me for his clothes:
a white shirt, a black tie,
black trousers and socks.
No need for shoes;
he was stripped
as I waited outside.

The shirt, which used to be a perfect fit
hung loose at the neck,
caved in at the chest;
the tie's knot was uneven
ridiculously large;
he would have said
something about that.

His Rotary watch (a birthday present
from mum twenty years earlier)
was unfastened from his hand
and given to me,
congealed, on a worn leather strap,
still keeping the beat,
leaving a white patch on his wrist.

Straw Hat
(Remembering mum 1925-2014)

Decades seemed to burst
from each crevice in the attic,
where the straw hat lay
on a dusty rocking chair.

Steel cobwebs chained
to breezes swayed,
like mama's hair
threads of shiny silver grey.

I remember her wearing it,
to hide from the sun;
now in permanent shade,
never to be worn again.

It's of sentimental value,
but who will care?
When I'm gone someone
will stuff it in a garbage bag.

And winds will howl
through fissured walls
like lone wolves,
that vanish in cotton mists.

The Last Advice

He stands there
like a Hollywood star
in a photograph
in his younger days.
A grandfather clock's pendulum
waves away the hours:
He whispered his last words:
Spend your life wisely,
it's the only defeat
you can inflict upon time.

After Surviving Cancer

To me it's heaven
When you can lie back
Looking at the passing world,
When you aren't in pain,
Afraid that you are dying.
Just lying down, eyes searching
Watching the colliding clouds
Hammering out light
Against this planet;
While the sun is holidaying
Refusing to give its warmth.
When there's nothing to think about
And you can spend your time
Imagining all your dreams come true.
Colours become brighter then
Even in the darkest hour.
Even when time eats up the days
Whilst you are obsessed
By your decreasing bank account,
Thinking about tomorrow;
When you might never see another sunrise,
When you already have all you need,
All the riches of the world
If you have your health.
If you can sleep peacefully
Without writhing in pain,
Once in a while dream again
Of whispering sweet nothings
To your first innocent love;
Running in feisty coloured fields,
Brimming with wild flowers
Without having to drag your body
Laden with diseases.

To ensure heaven is on earth
The future should always be your present,
Most important of all you must remember:
What you are now, I have already been;
Now, I am already what you shall become!

Unknown Grave

Peace reigns here
in cold stillness
on marble plaques
nibbled by the teeth of time;
among vagrant ghosts
watching our daily strife;
glancing from the outside
at our pain and grief
same they experienced
when they were alive.

Then in a wink of an eye
they ran away from it all
traveling fast into the light,
crossing beyond our rainbows
the bridges of no return.
A few more sunsets for us
will come in all their brevity,
for us each evening is a bonus
for them, it's eternity.

On the Beauty of Youth

These youthful moments are divine!
terminal beauty made sublime,
a unique artistic creation
sculptured by nature's inspiration,
men's heritage perfected by time.

A transient spell of youth's highlight,
when strength is at its very height
and beauty shines with all its might.
These youthful moments are divine!

But soon we realize our plight
glancing at the mirror in delight,
seeking the immortal pulsation
the elixir of life, death's evasion:
when soon youth fades out of sight.
These youthful moments are divine!

Imagination, Dreams
& Fantasy

The Mannequin
(Pantoum)

I thought the mannequin
Was throwing me a kiss
From its white pouting lips;
Virgin, that cannot speak or sin.

It was blowing me a kiss
After it had been stripped bare
A virgin, that cannot speak or sin;
Deadly still in its plastic skin.

After it had been stripped bare,
It was throwing me a kiss,
Deadly still in its plastic skin,
I fell in love with the mannequin.

The Vampire

Outside time it's cold
As the nocturnal creature freezes
In his white satin skin,
Transparent in mirrors
With gargoyle teeth
Awaiting his prey
In the dark shadows,
In the alleys, beneath bridges
Stalking humans for fresh blood,
The price for immortality.
Sadness is his only friend
Loneliness his lover;
He lives life without being alive
Immersed in his romantic destruction,
For he fears humans more
Than humans fear him.
With each kill he learns more
About the life he can never have:
Feelings, fear, pain, joy, anger, excitement,
The heroism to go on against all odds
Sometimes even knowing death is at the door;
The uncertainty of tomorrow
Of what life can bring.
Whilst he indulges in his immortality
Humans think of death as a relief
For after so many dreams shattered
And glory achieved, they hasten
To seek the Grim Reaper's final reprieve;
And whilst they rest in peace
He has to continue living forever,
To search and to seek.

Light after Dark

For us light after dark is not
like the aurora borealis;
it's not the day's beginning
on the edge of the horizon or on
a windowsill: an eye peeping over
a mountain, bloodshot from
too much opening and closing;
it's just a light within
that does not light up a room
but lights up a world
like no other light can do.

Light after dark is seeing
life's vitality through luminosity.
We are all children of light or darkness
born after sunset, or sunrise
when the day is on its way,
it's no matter we are blind
there is always a shade of grey.
It's all in the mind – if we lack one sense
it's likely another is sharpened instead,
and darkness is cut by a sword
that flashes in the night,
illuminating the mind from behind.

Light after dark is clean,
like cutting an eye-ball in half
without inflicting pain;
we cannot feel what we cannot see:
in one's life there is only one light within
bathing in a moon-filled pond
we see better with eyes tight shut.
But it doesn't matter, not really -
we recognize all truths far better
like they were written on stone,
and we can see with touch
all's hewn in our other senses;
therefore we do not crave for vision -
it comes to light after dark.

Reverie

I swayed in synchronisation
with the bows of an elm tree,
like a new born child in a cradle,
singing to a tuneless lullaby.
I was moved by a slow rhythm
the invisible hands of air,
the same that I breathed
and filled the universe.

I was shaken gently
to consciousness -
twitching from one dream to another;
sometimes I would smile,
sometimes I would cry
walking on disfigured leaves,
autumn's spring cleaning.

The night came
with shifting shadows,
filling fresh fuchsia pots
with rainbows.
It was as if I belonged here,
and was born of soil,
and could wither in autumn,
grow when flowers bloom.

My folded arms wanted
to prevent my heart
from letting it all go:
the jagged rustic stones,
grass washed by beaded dew
hanging like pearl earrings.
Little moths littered neon-lit lights.
Diamonds sparkled in the sky
illuminated my mind scanning my soul.

It was as if I had been blind all my life,
and what mattered then didn't now.
This darkness brought me to light,
I could talk with voiceless winds,
fertilise the soil with my sperm,
naked to the soul walk into a new world
shouting at the top of my voice:
This is I!

Inside the Bare Wall

Enter inside the bare wall
where the white room swallows shadows.
Close the file of your past
roll fast forwardly into the mist,
wait until it clears,
fade into the shade of trees.
Now, some long forgotten love
has fallen from your thoughts.
Ignore heartache - read Blake:
think, if only all you imagined
became real ...
.

Open your hands like a sail
let the breeze push you forward;
grit your teeth, the somersault complete.
Orchestrate your singing with birds,
do not be afraid to flirt.
Jot down the music in your brain
and juggle with the notes;
dance, twist like a whirlwind,
spinning and pirouetting.

In the quiet you can blink back
your tears, listen to yourself think.
Become a Buddhist, cultivate Chinese cactus
beat a rhythm on an African drum,
tam tira tam tam tam, tira tam tam tam ...
let your ears hear the jungle sounds,
until the damp humidity hurts
and stormy communications cease.
Now love will not need riches,
nor radiance in precious stones.

On Imagination
(Villanelle)

Imagination is a dream, an aesthetic land of never
food for the harmonious survival of mankind;
in wakeful dreaming it occurs with an everlasting fervour.

I consider it a state, a formidable quiet endeavour,
a thought provoking silence, deeply conceived in the mind;
imagination is a dream, an aesthetic land of never.

Mysterious, invisibly tangible like the scent of heather,
an internal rainbow that mesmerizes even the blind;
in wakeful dreaming it occurs with an everlasting fervour.

It forms part of our existence, it may even change the weather,
a power that makes men of the immortal kind;
imagination is a dream, an aesthetic land of never.

It is a capturing force, are fined hypnotic fetter
luminous like ectoplasm, and bright in its profound light;
in wakeful dreaming it occurs with an everlasting fervour.

Born as part of the human soul it takes shape or fades like ether,
Fascinating like the veritable essence of men's might;
Imagination is a dream, an aesthetic land of never,
in wakeful dreaming it occurs with an everlasting fervour.

The Dancing Bag

From stillness
    the gentle breeze
        inflates it with air,
            like a heaving chest
                lifting it in a spiral
                    of pirouetting leaves.

Then, the silent dance:
    the unfurling rush
swirling across,
upwards into twirled wrinkles
vacuumed into autumn's whirling winds;
this rustling flow takes off,
a ballerina performing a *grande jete.*

The Return to my House

She walked like she floated on air
And as she drifted past me I could smell
Her favourite scent of *Anais Anais*.
She was like a mythical 1920s model,
An animated portrait from an old book.
She passed by leaving me breathless:
She was there but I knew she wasn't;
Faded away in a blink of an eye,
A spectral figure I would have kissed,
If only for that single momentary bliss.

The wind inside the empty house sobbed
Convulsively still grieving her passing;
I never thought she would leave so quickly:
She stopped, looked back, it was my mother:
Elegant and beautiful as in the grey old photos
With her contagious smile of happiness.
And I was there too, a child holding her hand
Looking up at dad, proudly walking in between them;
Then dad took my other hand and together
They lifted me off the ground with a hurrah;
We laughed as my feet were dangling in mid-air.

I came across the mirror in the hall, looked inside;
There was no child, only an older version of myself:
Like Dorian Gray, I thought I couldn't age
But the image was now that of an old man.
I woke up just like when I was a boy,
Slowly half opened my eyes after a dream
Which I didn't want to come to an end.
There was no aromatic scent of brewing coffee,
No warmth of the rays of the sun on my bed.
It was dark, cold, and I was no longer a child:
Like a flash; that's how fast life passes us by.

The Ghost in the Ink Pot

The ghost in the ink pot
guided my hand
into the yellow light
of the desert,
then into the mirage
where the water
welled in my eyes
like a fountain
of crystals.

Suddenly I was
outside a world
of dimming lights
where the sun was masked
by damask,
and when it tired
simply laid down to rest,
cooling its fury
into the sea
sizzling as it sank.

.
The ink pot's ghost
leaves his mark
like the Scarlet Pimpernel,
in pulsating handwriting
in words from within;
flowing senseless,
or meaningful,
with calibrated rhythm
or rhyme, like music
sound spilling,
splitting silences.

The Illusionist
(Villanelle)

Let me dream about a quiet world of my own
Where mortals do not fret sickness or disease.
Do away with death and the marbled tomb stones!

A new world of tranquility where winds are blown
From unpolluted seas to a dying breeze.
Let me dream about a quiet world of my own.

About an everlasting wish of mine alone,
When I die, no earth shall fill my mouth's last wheeze.
Do away with death and the marbled tomb stones!

Eternally word-prone, rhyming each and every tone,
When solitude will lie with my soul in perfect ease.
Do away with death and the marbled tomb stones!

Youth shall reign, old age becomes a prohibited zone,
Unknown to men, sorrow will forever cease.
Do away with death and the marbled tomb stones!

And even death would be like a dream and a yawn,
An everlasting, unceasing relief to my grief.
Let me dream about this quiet world of my own
Do away with death and the marbled tomb stones!

Muse

When silence prevails
Bringing to a close
The sorrow and dismay
Of each and every day,

Leaving the heart at peace;
Let the mind wander a while,
The thoughts diffuse
Into the arms of muse:

There stay for a while
Let your mind astray,
Into its symphonic dream
Far from this dismal vale.

Love

Conquest

In my sleep I had an aching head drumming
out a nightmare of a conquest I was supposed to have made:
I had met Eva in a pub, her jet black hair gathered on one side

her intense blue eyes and long eyelashes rubbed against her
arched dark brown eyebrows,
her long legs were crossed, one more elevated
to show her sexy suspenders.

My eyes scanned through the unholy mist of cigarette smoke,
the air was thick with rancid breath from the many
alcoholic contenders:
when all of a sudden I was awakened in my bed.

Lying quietly by my side was my dinner date.
I was sober, my eyes clearer, I could see her sun-tanned curved body
beautiful, half naked, half covered by white silky sheets.

In the darkness, the sudden waking had opened my inner eyes,
immediately laid before me this harsh reality
and as I perceived her through the room's obscureness,

the dream, the magic, *'love'* became warped,
slowly took the shape of animal behaviour, turned into
a dreadful foreboding,
the notion that she was no more than a corpse without feelings.

I had desired her from the first moment I laid eyes on her
but now when my head was no longer swimming in booze,
without make-up, perfume, her voluptuous lips devoid of lipstick

all the craving and desire that had inflamed me,
to possess her was all in the black lacy lingerie laid carelessly
on the chair still dripping wet from the sweat

after our lustful wrestling love match before
our fiery passion exploded and was consumed by intoxication,
before sleep dug deep into our youthful sexual desire.

Now as she lay there, her breasts flat against the mattress,
into an unshapely mass of accumulated years and used God knows
how many times to lure men like me into an illusion mistaken for love;
the triumph of my *'conquest'* lay there, as a delusion,
snarling and snoring at the pillows.

Platonic Love

Beautiful as a Greek statue,
Her jet-black hair hung in satin long curls
Eyes beaming wide like a black onyx.
Only her voice spoilt the synchronization
Of this artistic creation:
It was coarse, masculine.

Married but naïve,
She was a virgin in more ways than one.
Never had a proper orgasm,
Simulated in a forced effort to express
Pleasure merely from a sense of duty.

She was stuck in stagnant boredom,
Often reflected in her nail biting habit,
As she watched with dreamy eyes
A colourless world go by
Beneath her confined balcony.
It was at times like this, their eyes met,
Fleetingly, in one single passionate glance
That often took their breath away.

That was all there was to their love affair.
It was enough; their eyes said everything
From poetry to pornography.
When she parted her lips, he parted his
And their tongues spoke in flicks
Triggering silent conversation.

Their love was condemned to make-belief,
Turning their heads away
When their eyes were about to speak;
When their smiles almost risked
Their hands waving kisses,
And their sighs were about to become
Too loud and clear to hide.
This love was different from many others,
A love so perfect, it could not survive.

Fleur
(Shakespearean sonnet)

I was a child when I first fell in love
though immersed as you were in vanity,
I had visions of magic and mystery;
so vivid full of illicit desire.

But now time has fled, and I know not where:
our promises - castles in the air,
made in the bedroom, when trembling fingers
explored our naked shame - we lingered.

I traced your curves with breathless lips,
called your sexy name a hundred times in vain.
You only used to laugh at me and feign
not to hear when I asked you to marry me.

You dipped your claws deep in me unfazed,
yet your cold blue eyes could not meet my gaze.

Our Maid Claire

Her long smooth legs were to die for.
When she came home, she always sat on the sofa
Crossed her legs and sipped her lemonade.
August then became even more of a sizzler
As her tongue licked her sensuous lips.
I imagined her every body language move
To be telling me silent sweet nothings;
And the rest of the world around didn't exist.
In contrast to her worn out hands and nails
I imagined her bare elegant thighs
In lacy black lingerie on our first wedding night.
Each time my thoughts made me drool,
She seemed to notice my lustful stare
And in exchange she crossed her legs again,
Slowly, so I could define the details in between;
Stark naked like my soul, I felt my heart was laid bare.
Every week until she came, I dreamt about her in my sleep
As often as I could, closing my eyes to imagine
And each time she was unmistakably there,
Voluptuous as ever, looking straight into my eyes.
Then one day my dreams became reality:
Claire came early as it was shopping day for mum.
I was in my bath gown still shaving before breakfast;
There was a knock on my door - it was her.
She came in and asked me for a cigarette, then a light;
Next, she was in my arms on the longest kissing quest
And our tongues needed not search for words;
As my hands explored her body, we fell back into reality.
Claire was supposed to be married within two months
We thought our love for each other was only lust:
I was a dreamer and she was young, both naïve,
Building our castles in the air, aspiring for a miracle.
As we slipped out of each other's arms we learned
We lived in an unforgiving world that discriminates
Between race and class. Claire was just our maid.

Forbidden Love

When they made love the first time
He never thought she'd walk away;
In his mind it was: *until death do us apart*.
When she wiped his sperm from her hand
It was the most intimate thing;
And when he helped her undress
All her secrets were laid bare:
Her smooth white skin,
The smell of *Chance Chanel*.
Her caress was a heart stopper
Their sighs, they could never stifle,
No wall was thick enough to smother.
That summer he lived through a dream,
Her light brown hair flowing over naked shoulders
Partly shading her perfect round breasts:
Her passionate kisses, soft, endlessly long
Sucked his heart his very soul;
Never again has he made love like that.
Each time it was like a first time
The experience was divine.
They were both young, thought they'd never part
There was like a certainty in their hearts;
Their love had come like in a fairy tale
During the college literary evening;
At the reception when their eyes met,
It was like they were the only two remaining
Amid a chaotic world.
Nothing could go wrong, their love was sealed.
As the years passed, they fell apart,
She left him to find another;
So did he move on from days of innocence.
Perhaps what they had was too close to a dream
Immature, afraid, they ran from each other.

Endless summers

How I dream about us going back in time
to those endless summers,
when time seemed to stand still,
as if waiting for us to catch up;
and when we watched sunsets
they were like fired mirrors
full of our passion and desire.

Then, it was forever, or so it seemed;
there were no signs of pain or fear,
both of us sweated for want of each other
our fingers slipping often into the unknown,
exploring forbidden crevices …
hoping these were the ultimate moments,
until we lay side by side breathless
trying to come to terms with what seemed
lawless, immoral, or even a crime;
our love was berserk.

I remember you in your tight blue shorts
which you wore so teasingly to provoke
showing off your suntanned curves.
You are a memory like an indelible portrait
only yesterday was twenty years ago.
Now, I wonder about your satin black hair,
if it still flows down to your naked waist,
if you still swing your head from side to side
like a flowing samba rhythm?
Often, you used to catch me
from the corner of your eye
and you would sadistically smile,
with your delicately thin fingers
pull your hair to one side
letting it flow onto my bare chest.

Then, I inhaled your perfume
as if it were the essence of life,
an elixir of immortality
never daring to wash it off
until you returned, night after night
in secrecy and silence,
while shushing my enthusiasm,
afraid our love would fade like the porcelain moon
in which we basked so often,
until it turned invisibly pale.

No one knew of our secret love then,
of our illicit desire to rest in each other's arms
spending those youthful nights,
until they turned grey with age.
When we touched, it was like an electric shock,
I often thought our hearts beat so fast
the thumping would give us away.
Your sighs and my sighs seemed so loud,
too loud to stifle into the darkness.

Until the land around us caved in
and we broke apart into divided worlds.
How I would like us together to go back in time -
if it was not for the fear we would linger on
perhaps, even choose different paths, different ways
never to return, never to be what we are today.

we both got what we had dreamed about
and ate each other to the bone.
Unconsciously we saw through life
and discovered a shade of grey.
Then, rains fell abundantly outside
and lightning tore us apart.

Bovary

She wore a see-through dress
and for the first time I saw
her red lingerie flashing danger.
She was like Madame Bovary.

I thought about starting afresh
without the passionate
obsession for her cleavage.
I dreamt of being in love.

The wine tasted better now.
I reeled on my feet
as I tried to get to the door.
My eyes burnt with mists
of cigarette smoke.

My feet felt like lead
waddling through sand.
The air was dense, I felt like
a terrorist trying to survive
through tear gas.

Love among the Debris

When December comes round
It is inevitable not to think of you
Of the greatest love saga ever told;
How you met my dad in WWII
And fell head over heels in love.
You were looking out from a window
Hidden in a narrow lane.
Your family had taken refuge there
From the relentless bombing raids,
Then, in the dead quiet, footsteps
Advanced one hot summer's day.
They were special footsteps
Of boots only soldiers wore.
Your sharp intuition urged you
To go out and have a look:
So you peered down your window
At a young soldier casually passing by:
He wore a smart kaki uniform
With the King's Own Malta Regiment badge.
And as he marched from shade to light
The badge with the eight pointed cross
Glistened half blinding your eyes.
It must have been a heavenly sign!
The amazing thing: he looked at you
With his huge brown eyes:
You often told me: *They were to die for,*
Then he gave you a dazzling smile.
And both of you seemed to know
This love was magical and sublime,
There to last for your entire life time.
When you returned inside your room
Your mind was all made up,
You made a promise to yourself:

If I don't marry him, I'll hide my love so deep
Nights will be longer - lovesick I'll never sleep!
And time and again he returned
Marching smartly down your street,
Every day it was the same routine:
Each time, his eyes said the same thing:
His lips formed the words: *I love thee!*
And in exchange you blew him kisses.
Then one day my soldier didn't visit:
In the street, there was a shocking quiet
As bombs exploded in the distance
Close to where my love was stationed.
The next day you went to the police
To check the list of fallen men,
But alas you suddenly remembered
Your love to you still had no name.
One morning the heavy footsteps came
Your dreamy eyes opened wide:
Instead another soldier came;
Walking beneath your window:
Are you Maria Aurora?
To which you so eagerly replied: *Yes!*
My handsome friend, the other soldier
Wants to ask you out but is too shy to do so,
So here I am to do it in his stead:
And hope together you can defy
The odds against you in this crazy world!
You wiped the tears from your eyes:
Your voice emotionally shaking:
Of course, I will, but what's his name?
The soldier removed his cap and bowed:
Vincent. He asked around to find out yours
And here I am acting like a Cupid,
Hoping my arrows have hit the target
Making my embarrassment worth its while!

Then the soldier mounted his bike:
And gave a long low whistle
Until in the silence came the familiar
Sound of heavy marching boots
And dad was there, his usual self:
With his dazzling soapy smile
And eyes to die for!
As you walked down the narrow street
The shades closed on your silhouettes,
Forming a single shadow.

First Night

How I still remember you
now as you cross my path
swaying your tall elegant body
your hair in pony-tail beating a rhythm
like the last samba we danced in Brazil

how your flanks still move
and I thought all was forgotten
for even now your buoyant breasts are still
the same where I had buried my blushing face
before you mounted my inexperienced erection
and rode me into light and dark
until I was dry and sweating
and after couldn't stop wanting you

how we groaned in ecstasy and I thought
this love was surely eternally sealed
and I could not forget
my heart refused to obliterate this memory
until I saw you flirting with another
whispering sensuously your tongue probing his ears
as you had done on our first night

how my heart missed the rhythm
and my chest ached from affliction
and to this day though I've ridden
to many a light and dark
I still remember.

The Girl on the Gozo Ferry Boat

Her stare into a void of blue,
a sea of salt, breezes blown,
unceasing, wave after wave of white foam.

She stood there,
a magnificent specimen of the human race,
half naked, suntanned flesh,
hips bare, curves showing
each time teasing winds rose.

Her face, shadowed profile,
her gloomy pensive mind,
withdrawn, aloof,
in search of something, happiness?
Joy is an elusive dream.

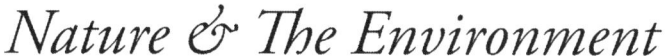

Nature & The Environment

House Demolishing

The intermingling loud breathing of life has stopped.
Within the silence the dust particles are invisible.
All wooden window shutters are closed in loud deafening stillness.
The babies have stopped crying, the cradles gone,
only one remains tilting on three legs,
the second eaten by woodworm rotting in a pile.
The mid-wives are old, no longer in fashion
retired in some forgotten residential home,
or buried in unknown churchyards showing only
their birth dates and dates of their demise.
Pregnant women now give birth in hospitals or in pools.
Then blood was hidden, the umbilical cord cut neatly;
the laughter, the excitement, the screaming.
Marbles no longer rolled nosily down the stairs
trapped within coloured rainbows in transparent glass.
One remains resting at the foot of the steps
embedded in dust, grey dirt accumulated over years.
The eyes of the people, now ghosts are sightless
gazing sadly on all these memories captured in time.

Its end is near, velvet red curtains drawn;
creviced walls humid green, paint cracked, faded,
discoloured, lifeless: once the owners' pride,
when they had carefully designed each room for each child:
fuchsia pink for the girls and sky and dark blue for boys.
Now all is suddenly quiet – only lamenting emptiness
a shrieking space remains, no lights, no electricity,
a single broken chandelier hangs on its rusty blooded chain
like a desperate man who had hung himself
to end it all before the Grim Reaper came for him.
Foot prints only mark the dusty marbled tiles
the wax and shine are gone forever from its eyes,
like a sun that has set and will never rise.

Then the deafening noise outside, the trembling explosion,
as the giant iron ball struck the walls of the house mercilessly
and it heaved its last long agonizing sigh, then collapsed,
in a mass of gory debris within which so many people lived and died
so many life sagas, tears, joy moments of glory, moments of strife.

The Dandelion Seed
(Petrarchan sonnet)

This single parachuted seed descends
softly swiftly in the parched garden soil
to flower, live, die, join the earthly toil.
This single parachuted seed transcends
all meaning of existence. Freshly blends
into a coloured world full of turmoil.
It defies all odds, makes the mind recoil
from its amazing and resilient strength.
It will grow then inevitably die,
to leave little or no trace on earth
of it ever having been. Just like us,
that strive until our demise.
Within this seed there is no pain of birth
at death, it simply turns to dust.

L
e
a
f

Just as a leaf
clings to a tree,
men cling to life;
when winds blow
with all their might
this boneless skeleton
shakes, falls to the ground;
just like men
when their time is done,
it withers into a netted web;
decays, dissolves,
into the fertile earth
giving birth
and breath
to a
new
l
i
f
e.

Poppies are not Even in Dreams

Multitudes of red poppies
open and close gaping at the wind;
like hungry lips wanting to be kissed.
Twilight steals the breeze
mobilizing cloudy shadows,
over tons of concrete,
a lifeless sea of grey micro apartments.
The scarlet tapestry sways to nature's rhythm,
like blood oozing from a giant wound -
now buried beneath new housing estates.
The sun is no longer visible as it sets
behind the high-rise buildings
and the night cannot be trusted.
Children are awake after 8p.m.
bored in their claustrophobic cages.
Soon these poppies
will not even be in their dreams.

A Mosquito's buzzing Birth

Buzzing it slipped out almost transparent
from beneath azure space;
razzing at its inability to fly

it fizzed with long proboscis,
beyond the day's quivering laze,
dazzled by cascading colours:

its vibrant jazz increased
it zigzagged
like a Harrier jet racing its engine:

then, as if it remembered
it zipped above water,

zapped out into space
with a fulminating blaze,
that was soon part of an orchestrated buzz.

Apocalypse

The gale-force wind is like a banshee chorus
Whines, whooshes through the concrete jungle
Whips the bashing blue sea roaring white foam,
Froths beneath, thrashing the solitary green boat
Soon crushed into a mash, blown to smithereens.
The turbulent clouds hide the sun's blushing face
In shame for all the sins committed by men,
Until roads are ripped by a river of bloody mud.
This is the last storm casting off its polluted slough
To the consternation of a helpless watching world.
All evil done to nature because of human greed
Now retaliates with merciless chaotic vengeance.
Men are devoid of any spirit of love and peace
Virtues departed on some long forgotten time train.
The end is here, all souls are sucked into a vortex
Swallowed by the gaping mouth of the grim reaper.
The air is clear after years of inhaling red mists,
Like scented perfume cuts deeply into the nostrils
Relieving to the lungs breathing their very last.

Sunrise of a Fishing Village

The fishing village comes to life
at the first light of dawn
with *Pawlu**, the fisherman shouting:
Lampuki Friski, Hajjin, Hajjin*!
Scaring away the last shadows
as they are sucked back into the pebbled beach
where they run, scurrying away
to hide with the crabs in dark crevices.

The radio news is all about politics
how one MP denigrated another;
how a burglar burst into a house,
and strangled an elderly woman.
Today the burglar is a repented poet
free as the wind and back in circulation.

Pawlu hollers in his high pitch voice:
Lampuki friski, Hajjin, Hajjin!
It's all about the fresh *lampuki, vopi or sparli**,
it's all about the bulging bright eyes,
glaring up from amongst the deep green seaweed.
The fresh smell of the sea and the salt,
his *luzzu*, Santa Maria**,
the fishing lines that earn him his living.

*Fresh Dolphin Fish, alive, alive!
*Lampuki (Dolphin Fish) Vopi (Bogue), Sparli (Annular Seabream)
*Traditional colourful Maltese fishing boats

Who cares about politicians and their lies?
Who cares about all those self centred snobs
who have never seen Pawlu's fresh *lampuki*?
It's all there, the truth you want to know,
the life you want to live, its true meaning:
a sun rising over the sand pebbled bay,
red in its shy apologetic face,
with each new day of human warmth,
as the shiny armoured fish quiver
in the torn wicker basket,
bliss captured in a time capsule.

Dr. Raymond Fenech

My Village Once a Safe Haven

Sunset bent over the horizon
into the poppy-filled virgin field
orange rays magically unfolding
on a child blessed by innocence
walking into the fading dream
through Swieqi Valley.
Now as a grown man
I walk in this same place,
a cemetery of urban concrete;
where apartments loom high
forbidding the day's light
from reaching smaller dwellings;
grey shadows touch the sky, stand
on tarmac-ridden roads,
sojourns for stressed aimless souls.

Gone is the smell of blood-red soil
wet from the first Autumn rain,
the ever changing coloured chameleons
that crossed my path in slow motion,
in the quiet vales and fields,
the green striped caterpillars
before they wove themselves into cocoons;
the farmhouses with their barking dogs,
the cocks' morning wake up calls,
fresh eggs sold from brown wicker baskets
white or tan - a dozen for a sixpence.

Twilight's tinkling bells have lost their chime
and few of the faithful go to the chapel
where I spent many a day as an altar boy.
Fr Eugene's gentle smile comes to mind
as I poured rose wine into his silver chalice:
then back home to a nightly quiet sleep
where I would fall into deep slumber,
to the whispering murmur
of my parents reciting the rosary.

Everything then was like magic,
when children were taught
they were brought into this world
from far unknown lands.
I was told I came home one stormy night,
on a powerful sailing ship
steered by the great Columbus himself.
All good people went to heaven,
the bogey man carried away naughty children
and ladybirds were a sign of good luck.

We stored our dreams
in castles made from carton boxes:
time did not run away from us then,
it slowed giving us more hours of play,
allowing us to indulge in our innocence our
carefree life full of health and youthful ways.
Summers seemed forever and ever.
Then came the new evil generation,
with no boundaries, principles or values
only greed for money, a wave of destruction
obliterating all in its path.
That's when time ran away from us
turning our fabled dreams to nightmares.

All the wild life has gone away
frightened by the demolition demons
as hundreds of quaint houses fell.
Apartments mushroomed everywhere
on black polluted roads,
built upon our blood lipped poppy fields;
the horizons disappeared from view
and there were no more idyllic sunsets.
Mornings turned into soot-ridden mists,
and all the quiet became relentless chaos
of a city that had no right to be here.
My village is now a red-light district
infested by binging zombies and vagrant criminals.
The sea in the bay is a shiny black
of multi-coloured oil spills;
the fishing boats have sailed never to come back.

Cobwebs

Cobwebs glitter in the dark;
when the moon lights up
we walk right into their trap:
they bend and finally break,
until this satin chain
of spider strength disintegrates.

Such delicate power
causes unexplainable fear,
a shock to our system,
a persisting phobia
so we destroy the netting
of the arachnid species.

Yet we are on top
of the food chain;
we bully like titans,
the mythical giants
as we walk rough shod,
creating havoc, destruction.

The spider will weave
its crystal webs tonight,
capture its prey no doubt.
We are the cyclops of today,
the spider, Ulysses of tomorrow,
our defeat is on its way.

Demolition

The long sinewy arm
striped its stone white skin
pealing it down to bare bone.
Sinister clouds of dust
engulfed the rose-pink sky;
and still shaking with shock,
the two remaining houses
quivered next to their fallen partner.

Like an old lady
it had heaved its last historic breath;
before deflating it collapsed to rest.
History is often made from grave mistakes:
for children to read about
before becoming an urban legend.

The house is now gone,
its ghostly outline shimmering
only visible to those who knew it.
When the dust-filled air cleared
the present threw its entrails into the past;
it was just another day gone by.
No one remembered the lives lived
that had once vibrated with emotion
inside this old house once full of light.

Dreaming About My Home Village

Every time I dream
I drift to my home village
when in those quiet days
only the church bells chimed
the waking of a new day;
when the streets were a holy place
where children could play safe;
only the bogeyman was a danger.
Quaint coloured houses
in yellow, green, blue or fuchsia pink
had little wooden windows,
and with each rise or fall of the sun
they seemed to wink at me.

Every time I dream
there's my little house
with its shutters green
overlooking Spinola Bay;
the gentle swishing waves
on its pebbly shores
welcomed with each dawn.

When the fishermen's wake-up calls,
*hajjin, hajjin, friski hajjin**
were our natural alarm clocks.
And when the sun plunged headlong
into the purple blue abyss,
their multi-coloured *luzzi**
chugged rhythmically out to sea;
darkness then was still safe
and door keys were left in the locks.

Alive, alive, fresh, alive!
Colourful Maltese fishing boats

Every time I dream
I see winter as it used to be:
when the wind composed love songs
to our virgin olive and carob trees;
children played in the streets
their pink flushed faces smeared
with muddy soil from freshly fallen rains
that leaked from farmers' fields,
where potatoes, fresh broad beans
grew in multitudes like children's dreams.
In those days when Christmas came
Christ was the protagonist;
the soul came first
and all was bathed in haloed light.
There was no revelling,
joy was at midnight Mass
in the traditional altar boy's sermon.
Then all house decorations had cribs
with soft lights and freshly cut pine
that made Christmas aromatic.
In Spring, winter slipped quietly away
replaced by a soft caressing breeze;
spring was visible on the wayside
where swaying red poppies bled
like a glowing healthy face.

Every time I dream
of my little village
there are no concrete prisons,
endless rows of new apartments,
soulless eyesores and tasteless buildings
polluting the quaint fishing village.
There are no fumes from belching buses,
or noise pollution besieging the quiet;
the frantic pace of life, which stole
all blissful moments from our lives;
then, we could hear ourselves think.

When I dream now,
it's all a nightmare
about an unrecognizable town,
and traffic lights flashing frantically,
where a warning sign reads:
Please turn back
you are now entering
a chaotic war zone!
Some call this progress
but it is only so for the privileged few,
those who have never dreamed
nor loved, cared or lived
in the once sleepy village of St. Julian.

Dr. Raymond Fenech

The Electric Storm

*(Nominated for the Pushcart Prize
by Poeticdiversity Literary Magazine, Los Angeles, USA)*

Tonight the sky is an electric dream
flashing its giant camera with all its might
with an unceasing photographic mania.
Children hide their heads under the pillows
and parents pray to St. Barbara*
from fear of such magnificence.
Electric dreams pass into impregnated skies
full of young fantasies in unexplored oceans
where many a Columbus's hopes sank.
November is the month of the dead,
when flower shops sales are at their peak
when Catholics burn thousands of candles
hoping to save souls, even those already lost.
And this feast of lightning sounds
like sacrileges fireworks, an angry God
chiding us for behaving like the Pharisees
giving us an opportunity for eternal life.

*When there are thunderstorms it is a common tradition of the Maltese,
especially of the elderly, to pray to St. Barbara for protection from the
damage that lightning can inflict on their homes.*

The Failed Summit with the Rain

This morning I wanted to speak with the rain;
          Tickle the winds,
Ruffle the clouds with a broom,
Clean the air full of misty fumes,
          So life can be lived
And flowers can bloom.
Where arid lands and buildings stand,
          I would demolish and replace
With fields, farms and trees,
And carpets of emerald green.

This morning I wanted to speak with the rain;
          Touch the air,
Caress the waves with naked hands,
Clean the shores from deadly fuels,
          So nature can survive
And extinction of any species banned.
Where there are ruthless men
          Who think they are like Gods
Sentence them to death;
          Their spoils put on a stand
With large notices saying, Beware!
If you do not wish to lose your head!

This morning I wanted to speak with the rain;
          Shower beneath its natural flow,
Breathe again odourless perfumes,
Clear the world from politics,
          So man can be human
And greed for wealth prohibited.
Where there are politicians
Who are for themselves, not for country

Banish them to concentration camps
                Their lives auction as slaves
Lock them up among psychopaths and murderers;
Their names change to numbers, record all their actions.

This morning I wanted to speak with the rain;
                But the rain is acidic,
It burns, stains and has lost its virginity;
This water no longer reflects the soul
                Of earthly elements;
It has lost its power of cleansing,
Wherever there's men it seeks his destruction.
        I would say more, but my words would end me in jail
And fields, farms and trees,
Will always remain where they are, in my dreams.

The Mountains of Mourne (Ireland)

The
sheep
stand
dotted grey
against a mantle of green.

The tips of mountains
hidden-like,
Jack climbing the bean stalk,
breaking
through clouds; mists, that hang over
from never ending skies,
menacing, threatening rains
that never seem to fall.

The sheep dogs break loose, yelping
into a run, tongues hanging,
rounding up the phosphorescent sheep
as twilight comes
like a spectral myth of romance
eternal salmon pink
which has kept the night at bay, since
days of yore and legends.

Now, the sheep are all gathered
unlike my raving thoughts,
vagrant tramps of mischief and wonder.
I leave these mountains
blushing with rhododendrons afraid
I will die
and never be back here again.

Bonjour St. Hipployte (South of France)

There is a silent hum in the grey mists
hovering low over the little *cled,*
the air is a lifeline of pure oxygen
that smells like fresh raw eggs.

Squirrels like furry arrows,
dart softly across the chestnut;
shadows crawl lazily across the garden
over water mirrors,
like the ghosts of all those
who made history on this silk farm.
It's sad this quiet cannot be shared.
Only wild boars dare break
this silence into shards,
as they grunt their strength loudly
uprooting flower bulbs.

I nestled deep inside myself
but still couldn't find my soul.
It must have flown, escaped,
not wishing to return home.

Over the Rainbow

When I walked up *The Gardens'* hill
to watch red lights fade in distant fields
hand in hand with my Aunt Mary,
it was like walking over the rainbow,
over a magical bridge to the Land of Never;
towards distant castles,
knights in shining armour on white stallions,
stomping the ground with their heavy hoofs
preparing to gallop to save damsels in distress.
In this part of the world injustice reigned
the poor and the weak struggled to survive
and lawmen only wrote legislations
in favour of the rich and powerful.
I wanted to believe these knights were there
to cut down evil men with their broad swords,
or run them through with their jousts.

Since my last walk up this hill
the sun's face is no more, the open space
walled up blocking its rays,
the fields converted into jungles of concrete.
The pebbled paths, the soil bulldozed away
and when darkness collapses from the sky
the ever vigilant eye has been blinded,
and the tarmacked lava has fossilized
the seeds of an array of wild plants,
which coloured this path in their multitudes.

The buildings scrape the sky injuring the clouds:
the land upon which they were built
full of ghosts of farmers who have passed
who have become part of the earth they once loved,
that stuck to the bottom of my Wellingtons in winter.
No more poppies dance happily to the breeze,
and summer fresh winds have turned into hot air
dense with polluted fumes and speckled dirt.
The recipe for corruption, greed, a soulless generation
dances to techno music and racket rap,
composed by disturbed minds inspired by Mephistopheles.

*Dolphin Fish. It is a very traditional Maltese dish, which most tourists would seek during August, September and October when the fishing season for this type of fish is at its very peak.

Remnants of St. Julian's Village

The old village used to smell
of fresh fish and sea lettuce,
of seawater stored in barrels
where fish were cleaned and washed.

The fishing boats are all departing
but not on fishing trips
to catch *lampuki,**
but on harbour cruises for tourists.

Ports are no longer made
from aging pebbles where crabs
used to build their den,
and little prawns tickled
children's toes as they cooled
their feet in the warm summer sea.
It's all luxurious yachts
flooded by artificial lights,
reserved only for the privileged few.
.

When the wind angers
the rest of the elements,
it's no longer like it's blowing kisses,
rather it's like it hisses:
The past has passed,
no place for the past ...

When the first rain falls,
the poppies and clover
will be gone from the fields
and more concrete cages built.
More trophies for the millionaires:
the red and green is only in traffic lights.

The Carob Tree

The air smells of pollution,
time rips the living and the dead.
There was a world once that loved
and was loved, and fresh fruit
was for everyone's taking.
There was always a harmless sun
behind coloured clouds.

Now the sun hurts the ozone.
Eyes close exploring narrow lanes,
lost in some forgotten valley
where a carob tree grows.
The car park is full and soon
the tree will be removed.

I wanted to come here again to feel
the breeze scented with jasmine,
that grows alongside the carob.
But now the jasmine's dried stalk
clings to the wall tied by cobwebs.
There's a stench of urine
and decaying human faeces.
No more will perfumed jasmine flowers fall
white-washing the soil.

Life is like an echo;
it starts strong then fades,
full of youth and old age.
No longer does the child
run with his dog at his side through
the swaying wilderness,
there is a highway in its midst.
Now, with the onset of darkness,
only my shadow is happily at play
immune to finality, but soon to fade.

To St. Julian

No longer does the hoarse fishmonger
shout at the crack of dawn – *Lampuki hajjin, hajjin!**
The voice has been drowned by pneumatic hammers
to make way for a new hotel that must kill competitors.
Fresh fish is only available in restaurant freezers.

I can still see myself catching caterpillars,
climbing almond trees at *Spinola* Palace gardens,
now raped by the erection of *Portomaso* apartments.
I watched them turn from cocoons into Cabbage White,
blew softly on their unfolding wings to dry.

Attired in fancy running lights
the village is fossilized beneath concrete cages.
Kids are now men and men have turned to compost.
We are shadows of moving clouds,
vanishing with gusts of wind;
like the old tramp with the lame dog,
the paraffin man who died of cancer,
and the young fisherman's son,
who hanged himself from the stairs' railings.

The night sky is clear from dust –
the hurricanes of falling debris subside
into a silence that is solely inside the heart;
the orange sunset is only in dreams.

Fresh Dolphin fish, alive, alive!

Totalitarian Democracy

*("All animals are equal, but some animals are
more equal than others." G. Orwell)*

My sanity is hanging
On a thin tread
Struggling to cope
With the weight;
It stretches, vibrates
Above turning tides
Angry foaming waves,
Reflecting the rays
From the red dot
Of a bloodshot eye,
Tired of burning
As it fades out of sight.
Each day, it dives deep
Behind the concrete
Into an unseen abyss
No longer into the sea.
Fine dust settles
On the window's edge
Polluted black:
We wash away
Scrub hard, to no avail;
No sooner we clean
It returns, we close an eye
Trying to pretend
That it's not there.
Air is no longer invisible
Soot bombards its space,
Fills our nostrils and lungs.
But there are no laws
Against legalized murder,

Justice sleeps comfortably
Surrounded by landscaped gardens,
Luxuries swimming pools
Inside its off the beaten track villa,
Where pollution does not affect
The rich and the corrupt
Who have usurped and robbed
Us of our healthy habitat.

A Requiem to a Millennium Spring

I want childhood spring to come back
To haunt me like those days
When clean breezes tickled my hair
From open spaces around the little bay.
Where the turquoise sea was still pure
From the oily crust fuelled surface.
When the wind could still be heard
Flowing through the yellow wood sorrel
Swaying in fields, dancing to nature's
Sweet symphonic cacophony.
Then I thought it would last forever.

Now, I cannot even see the sky
It's all grey concrete, the sunlight
Stolen away from the old quiet streets,
Where life flourished within humble abodes
Of people who embraced traditional values:
When Christian principles were non-negotiable;
Where money counted little and real men
Could watch sunsets through perfectly
Clear skylines quietly reciting the rosary;
While children dreamed sweetly
Falling asleep to their mother's lullabies,
Or listening to some long forgotten tale.
Nights stole in, closing on their innocence
As silently they floated into harmless dreams
Almost visible on their happy rosy cheeks.

Nothing then was impossible for people
Serenity and peace were available for free;
No one thought about too much wealth
Or anything that was not within their reach.
For they lived their simple lives happily:
And when it was time, they departed this life
As they lived, without much pomp, poorly but joyfully;
In exchange, they passed with a clear conscience
Free from the burden of having become rich
At the expense of everything and everybody else.
Those same streets now have become narrower,
Darker, and the shade in summers wreaks
Of mounds of restaurant garbage and polluted air:
Corruption is rife and the air stinks of evil.

And there is still no sign of the *patriotic politician*,
The unsung hero who doesn't fear to do what's right,
The man who upholds every citizen's rights,
Castigates those who abuse and rob their neighbours
Of the right to live in quiet and peaceful harmony,
In a debris and dust free environment;
Where trucks and tower cranes do not invade our streets
Endangering our lives and mental sanity.
Silence no longer exists, not even at night
And louts, yobs and criminals infest our towns
And justice is as corrupt as the police are clowns.

Dr. Raymond Fenech

Within the Edges of Mortality

This flower bursts open
Like a colourful firework,
Yellow in its humble beauty
Gulping sweat and tears
Never ravishing art and philosophy
Yet master of both and silence;
And the air full of its aura's energy
A smell that ravishes the nostrils
And thirsts parched tongues,
But what of this beauty
If it confines death?

Ballades & Legends

Paul the Meticulous Fisherman

Pawlu is-Sajjied,* as he was nicknamed was a quiet lad.
Every Sunday morning he would clad in a beige suit and tie,
shine his shoes with spit, like soldiers in the army.
He was neat, in fact his other nickname, *Pawlu l-fitt.* *
Meticulous in his work, he considered life was ridiculous.
His walk was a rhythmic sway of self confidence
stopping to observe the weather like all good fishermen.
It only seems like yesterday,
Pawlu was shouting himself hoarse: *Lampuki friski, hajjin hajjin;* *
no one realized he was in deep crisis, deeper than the sea
from where he caught us fresh fish every day.
His *luzzu,* * *Santa Maria* * was berthed at Spinola Bay,
now it's gone just like him leaving an empty space
with only a lonely buoy to mark its place.
Pawlu no longer shouts, *Friski, hajjin hajjin*:*
and the mornings are drear without his yellow smile.
When my dog ran out into the street last year
Pawlu gave chase and brought him back safe.
The Santa Maria was red, black and yellow,
painted in honour of St. Julian the village Belgian saint.
It would chug out from the bay, sometimes moon rising
every evening for summery decades, as many as I can recollect,
rippling through the reflected white light of a dimming sunset.
Then, he would whistle an unknown tune
until his silhouette became one with dusk.
He lived with his old widowed mother, *Giuzeppa;*
everyone knew she dotted on him, her only son.
One day she came back from early morning mass
and found him hanging from the neck.

Dr. Raymond Fenech

The rope was tied by a fisherman's knot from the stairs' railings.
The doctor came first, then *Dun Karm,** the Parish priest. *Pawlu*
left us suddenly without a warning sign;
now, he is only a ghostly memory
as the moon rises on an empty quiet bay.

*Pawlu is-sajjied il fitt (Paul the meticulous fisherman)
*Pawlu il-fitt (Paul the meticulous man)
*Luzzu (traditional colourful Maltese fishing boat)
*Luzzu, Santa Maria (the boat is named St. Mary)
*Lampuki friski, hajjin, hajjin. (Fresh Dolphin fish, alive alive)
*Friski, hajjin hajjin. (Fresh, alive alive)
*Dun Karm (Fr. Charles)

The Vegetable and Fruit Vendour

It was summer when *Zaren**, the vegetable fruit vendor, hollered
At the top of his piercing voice and the sunbathing lizards
Within the sun-scorched rocky vale ran into their obscure homes.
The women from the colourful houses thronged onto the street,
Queuing near his green horse driven cart, the large wheels
Rumbling on the pebbled slabs of the quiet fishing village.
I often accompanied my mother and for the white stallion, Polly
Bought a single red apple to offer to her drooling mouth;
Each time when she recognized me, she gently nudged my hand.
The vegetable and fruit vendour was an old man in a white torn shirt,
He wore a straw hat and a piece of rope for a belt; his son had died
On his sleeves he always wore a black band as a sign of mourning.
The choice of vegetables and fruit were few but always fresh
Every morning the cart wheels could be heard grinding painfully
Up the hill, Polly pulled the cart right up the street then stopped:
Zaren's voice shrieked out the names of the vegetables most fresh,
Then the fruits, then told the same story about his long lost son
Who departed this earth after battling two years with cancer.
It was always the same, until one day *Zaren* did not turn up,
The village waited in vain for his strident wake-up call:
It was said he had passed away while dozing under a carob tree;
Polly was found standing ready with harness and a full loaded cart
Bending over the vegetable fruit vendor who slept for the last time.

*Zaren is a shortened Maltese name derived from Nazzareno, meaning Nazarene

The Legend of Gomerino Palace

As I was swallowed by the darkened shades
The wintry fingers of that cold night
Pierced deep through my flesh to my spinal cord;
Like razors cutting the remaining light.
And I feared this place with all my might,
On remembering feudal times of long centuries gone by
When poor peasants toiled and slaved until they died.

I shivered as I thought of legends past
The ghosts that haunted here from long ago;
The evil that hid, lurking in the dark
Lying in wait to possess some innocent soul.
When nightly creatures deep from sleep arose,
Their susurrations sounding eerie and wild;
As I came to the gate, my heart went cold.

Now as the story of this palace goes,
Years back, five hundred years ago at least,
Lived a count who had imprisoned his son.
The poor boy was born half human, half beast,
Chained to the cold dungeon walls of the East
Far, far from everyone's sight, until that day
When the count died after a sumptuous feast.

In thick cobwebs encased, his son was found
Years later, by his heirs who came to stay.
They were horrified at the ghastly sight
Of the monster with gargoyle fangs decayed.
And they left, never, never to return.
To date none dare enter this accursed place:
It is said his ghost still lives on in his domain.

The Legend of the Red Dogwood

A legend speaks about the red Dogwood,
How during a certain crucifixion
So gigantic, tall like an oak it stood,
It served as a cross for His affliction.

This destiny worried the tree so much
That He sensed its unhappiness deep inside,
And assured it that He bore no grudge,
He said it would bear witness to his plight:

Never again will you grow huge and strong
From now, you will be slender, twisted and bent,
Your blossoms like a cross, two petals long,
Two petals short - pray mankind will repent.

In the very centre of the outer edge
On each of your petals, nail prints will appear,
Rusty brown, blushing, crimson, stained with red.
Far, far away from evil men must steer.

And in the centre of each of your flowers
Will be a crown of thorns for all to see,
Recalling this man and his last hours,
And you hence forth, from sorrow shall be free.

A Biography

The Old grandfather clock chimes the *Ave Maria*.
When his grandparents died the sound became a mental strain.
It was sold in an auction; he will never hear its refrain.

His uncle's summer residence was a lighthouse.
With his cousins, as a child, they chased the shadows away.
Dusk was an adventure; only stars lit their way.

For years, his father was a Franciscan novice. Sex was a sin.
Sunday mass with cousin Elsie was a passionate quest.
Hands folded, he reached with his fingers to fondle her breasts.

In South Africa, he lived in a hut with the poor.
It was at the peak of youth, when he was moving at full steam.
There, all hopes and aspirations vanished like a dream.

The house where he lived, where he would want to die
Smelt of the past, when all was well and he was young.
There, garden ghosts whispered advice in silent tongues.

When he was assigned to Bosnia, he became immune to fear.
Being a Red Cross volunteer required certain courage.
When it was over, he was no longer afraid of carnage.

He was thirteen and naked. He did not know he was being watched.
His cousin Ralph walked inside his bedroom like a streak.
His eyes spoke clearly. Ralph was strong and he was weak.

His first 'love' was homosexual. He was raped by pleasure.
When eighteen, Celia came giving him the first French kiss.
When his tongue inside her churned up juicy bliss.

Celia had the loveliest eyes he had ever seen.
Her lips sensuous, when she spoke his eyes filled with tears.
Her breath slid softly inside his ear like an elixir.

As a child, his favourite companion was a piece of cloth.
When frightened he covered his face keeping the world outside.
He grew violent. Tsaikovsky's 1812 was as if war was in his mind.

Personality disorder struck. He fought against himself.
Until reality and fear drove him insane.
A clock chimed the *Ave Maria*; he will never hear its refrain.

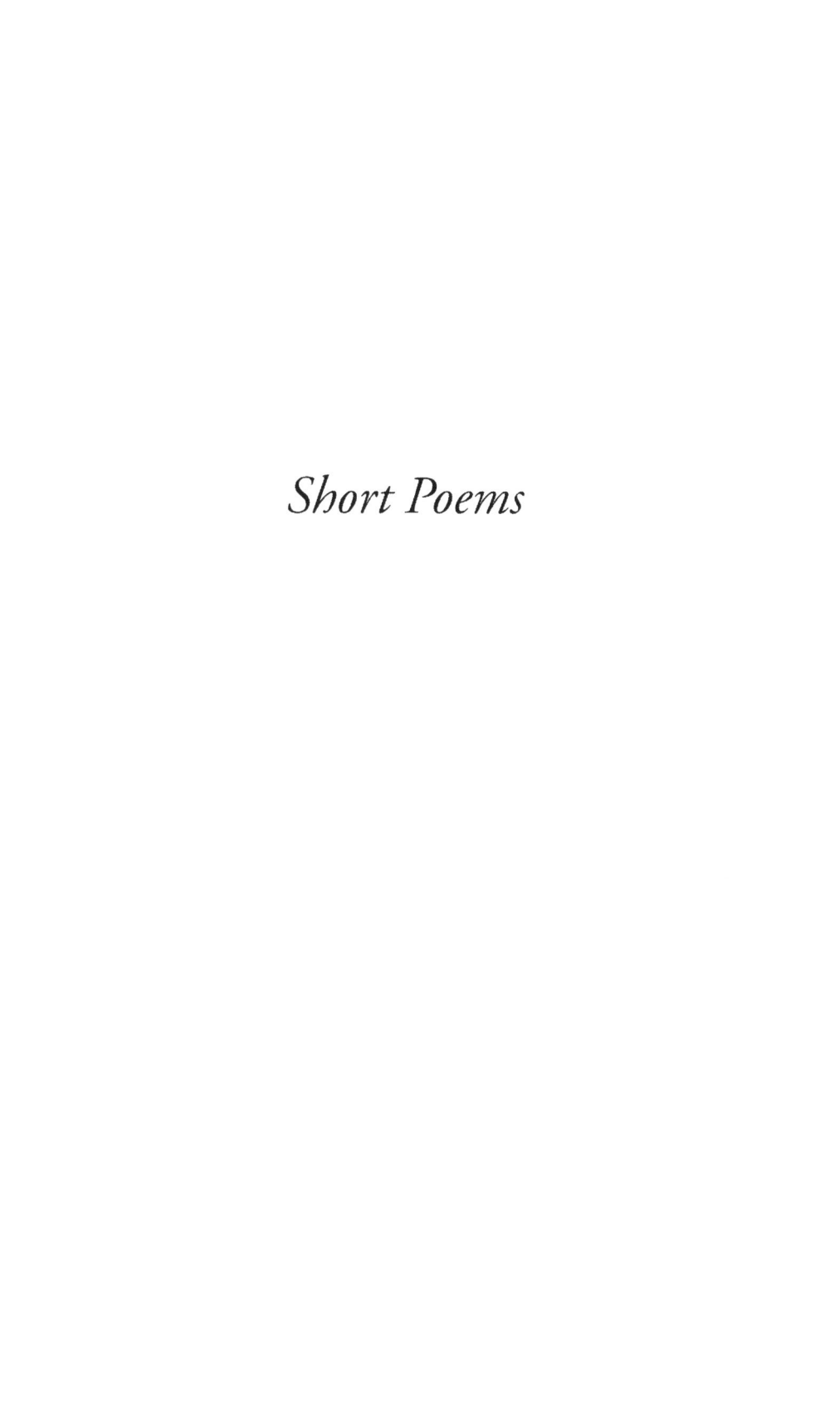

Short Poems

Dawn
(Japanese Tanka)

Night shades the long day
in a translucent red veil
turns from black to grey
until the sun's blinding rays
bring us back another day.

Waves
(Japanese Tanka)

Waves are torn apart
windsurfer riding the wind,
lightning strikes its path;
bent mast in hand at full speed,
like a brandished scimitar.

Jilted
(Japanese Tanka)

I saw you alone
gazing at Spinola Bay;
when still at my side
your love was also my dream,
before your vicious deceit.

Dr. Raymond Fenech

Innocence of Old
(Japanese Tanka)

Drenched in summer's light
children played in narrow streets
with coloured marbles;
innocence was at its peak
on their soft rosy cheeks.

The Concrete Jungle
(Japanese Tanka)

The sun dies slowly
only a shadow of what
it used to be then;
the once virgin land cringes,
beneath jungles of concrete.

Dr. Raymond Fenech

Voyage into the Light
(Japanese Tanka)

I laid in deep sleep,
dreamed of a long quiet road
leading to bright lights,
saw through closed eyes a passage
a peaceful silent demise.

198

Revisiting

I cannot help,
but recall
all sweet memories
as I stand alone
looking at the house
where I was born.

Medicine for the Mind

Imagination is what fulfills our minds
we use it to conquer grim reality
to keep us hoping to survive.

Falling in love

I fell in love a million times
day in day out
each time I thought:
This is the one.

From the Sea
(Japanese Tanka)

Born in salt water
Life was awakened in me
By the deep blue green;
The child grew into a man
Out of the cobalt blue sea.

Paying for Air
(Somewhere in the third millennium)

Once there was a man who was taken to court
For breathing all the pure air around him;
The law declares, by the judge he was told:
The air we breathe cannot be given for free,
For pollution has made it a rarity indeed.

Sensitivity

Man moves mountains
yet it takes so little
to move man.

The Beheading

Guillotined the sun loses its head
Condemned to daily death.
Thick blood blushes into red
Floods from blue to black instead.

A rare recurring colour mixture.
Mists smoke to a hazy standstill,
Light flashes on the windmill
Like a camera taking a souvenir picture.

Dr. Raymond Fenech

The King of Sorrow

When I was young I was a lad
I was so mad I could not think
why people seemed so very sad.
Now, old, of sorrow I am king.

206

Tomb Inscription
for Tommy 1975-1979

A huge tattered teddy bear
sat like a hairy guardian angel
braving the foul weather.
Written on the cold marble slate:
God, please take good care of our Tommy.

I wrote this poem on 1st November 1985, whilst visiting the Addolorata Cemetery with my colleague and senior photographer of The Times of Malta, Frank Attard. It was customary in those days for our newspaper to pay tribute to the feast of All Souls' Day by taking an unusual photo of a grave to create a caption story for the next day's edition. The grave we came across shocked me, when I noticed a giant Teddy Bear sitting on its newly laid marble and the tomb inscription in my poem, noting that some young couple had lost their child aged four years. But it was not just Frank and I who were overwhelmed and traumatized by this tragic scene: the following day many of our newspaper readers complimented the newspaper staff for the photograph. The scene remains indelible in my mind to this very day.

A Wistful Invader

Weary and tired of life
As I am
With problems to which I see no end
I try to smile:
But this lasts only for a while
Until sorrow wins again.

Silent Teachers

Stone walls cannot speak

but there is much to be learnt

from their silence.

Delight in Joy

Life is only tragic
If we pursue it thinking
Joy is part of its magic;
Happiness must be earned
So delight in it when at hand;
If for some reason it is lost
We must recover it at all cost.

Conflict

Man pines,
the brain reasons
debates with the heart.
Yet in conflict
both survive,
the perfect couple.
Decades melt into the space of time
until both together
pass beyond this mortal confine.

Inconsistency

Men are inconsistent
because life constantly changes
and so does their needs.

Sweet Memories

I cannot help,
but recall
all sweet memories
as I stand alone
looking at the house
where I was born.

Life

Human life
is like the oncoming waves
breakers against all odds.

They climb on the rippling sands
ebb away and fade
leaving little or no marks

in this great infinite space.

About the Author

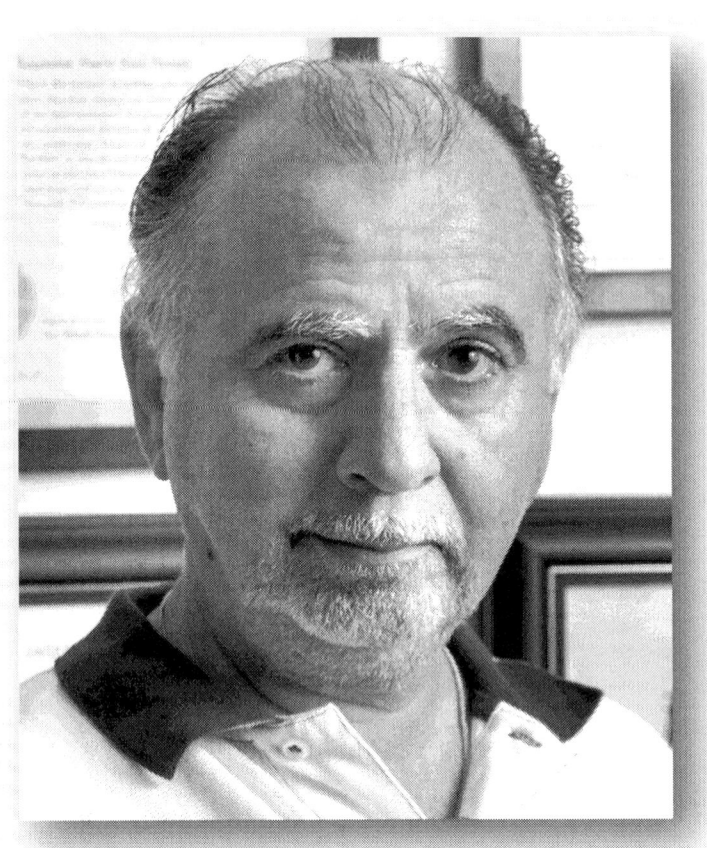

Born in 1958 in the small fishing village of St. Julian, Malta, **Dr Raymond Fenech** embarked on his writing career as a freelance journalist at 18 working for leading newspapers, *In-Nazzjon, Il-Mument, The Democrat, The Times* and *Sunday Times of Malta*. In more recent years, he edited two local nation-wide distributed magazines and founded and managed one of the largest in-house advertising agencies.

In 2003, the author was diagnosed with Hodgkin's Lymphoma and was temporarily forced to an early retirement. For nine months he was in hospital for intense chemotherapy treatment and on completion had a stroke. Miraculously, the author recovered well enough to get back on track and founded his own business in copywriting and PR.

Between June and November 2017, the author was nominated twice for the prestigious Literary *Pushcart Prize* in the USA by two different publishers. The first nomination came from the bi-lingual *Adelaide Literary Magazine* of New York and Lisbon after winning the 1st Prize in an essay competition with his story, *The Mysterious Priest* and in November he was also nominated for the same prize by the Los Angeles online *Poeticdiversity Literary Magazine* for his poem, *The Electric Storm.*

Fenech has two journalism diplomas, a Bachelor of Arts degree in creative writing and more recently obtained a PHD from UK-based educational institutions

He was awarded a scholarship in Writing Therapy by the *Creative 'Righting' Center, Touro College, Hofstra University*, New York in 2009 and was mentored personally by the founder director of the *National Association of Poetry Therapy*, USA, Professor Sherry Reiter. The author has completed several other specialized courses in various fields of writing and is a qualified journalist, copywriter and editor.

The author is also a certified paranormal investigator and has published research on the ghosts of Malta in the *International Directory of the Most Haunted Places* by *Penguin Books*, USA. Between 2006 and 2008, the author completed four courses in paranormal studies with *Flamel College*, USA and was awarded a diploma in paranormal studies by the same college for his 158-page illustrated thesis, *The Ghosts of York*. As a result during the same year, Fenech founded the *Paranormal Investigations & Research Foundation (Malta)*. The foundation's web site may be viewed at: www.pirfmalta.com/ In 2014, he completed a short course in parapsychology with the *Edinburgh University*, Scotland.

Ray is also listed as a professional copywriter with *The Copywriting Institute*, UK and recently completed a diploma course in Journal Therapy with the *UK College of Holistic Training*.

He is member of the *Canada Cuba Literary Alliance, Poezija Plus,* Malta, *The Institute of Copywriting*, UK, and *The International Ghost Hunters Society*, USA.

In the author's own words about poetry: *"I like to write poetry in a language everyone can understand, without mincing words, or losing my way in the obscure, or the abstract. Poetry from its very origins was intended to entertain the masses, even the illiterate. It is another*

form of communication and therefore each word has to be simple enough for the majority reader to understand. Like Hemingway, I think 'the most important equipment for a writer is a built-in, shock-proof shit detector', which can identify nebulous sentences. Readers usually want to associate themselves with the poet's feelings, but to do so they first have to understand his writing."

The Author published poems in several magazines and literary journals in 14 countries including, *The Envoy,* official newsletter of the *Canada Cuba Literary Alliance*, Canada, *White Ash Literary Magazine*, USA, *Boston Poetry Magazine*, USA *The Ambassador*, the official literary magazine of the *Canada Cuba Literary Alliance*, the newsletter of the *Professional Writers' Special Interest British Group MENSA*, UK, *Poetry Canada*, *Flaming Arrows*, Ireland, *Expressions Online Magazine*, Canada, *Quantum Leap*, Scotland, *Verses Magazine,* USA, *Electric Acorn*, Ireland, *Poetic Licence*, UK, *Poemata* the main poetry journal of the *Canadian Poetry Association*, Canada, *Juju Magazine*, Northern Ireland, *Other Poetry*, UK, *The Affectionate Punch*, UK, *Breakfast All Day Magazine*, France, the *Adelaide Literary Magazine,* USA and Lisbon, *The Quail Bell Magazine,* USA and *Phenomenal Literature*, India. Many of his poems have also been published in numerous poetry anthologies in Canada, the USA and the UK. Short stories and literary essays were also published in several other literary magazines and anthologies.

His latest books, *The Incident of the Mysterious Priest and Other Stories* and a new poetry collection, *Growing with the Shadows* will be launched shortly at the international book fair *Expo America* in New York.

The author will attend the fair to sign copies of his book at his publisher's book stand.

The opening of the fair is being presided by US Senator Bernie Sanders, a former professor of Literature and very popular in literary circles and activities.

Articles on various themes by the author were also published in *Renaissance Magazine*, USA, the *Globe Trotter Magazine, Living* 2000, *Island Life Visitor's Guide,* and *The Sunday Times Motoring Magazine* Malta.

He is listed in the *International Who's Who of Poetry and Writers,* UK, *The Poetry Kit Online*, UK, the *Who's Who of Maltese Authors and Poets Directory* and the *Encyclopedia of Post-Colonial Literatures in English* edited by Eugene Benson, University Professor Emeritus of English, *L.W. Conolly Vol 1,2,3,* which includes more than 1,600 entries written by more than 600 internationally recognized scholars, and explores the effect of the colonial and post-colonial experience on literatures in English worldwide. In this encyclopaedia reference is made to his first two poetry books, *Within the Edges of Immortality* (1994) and *Poignant Voices* (2000). A permanent biography of the author was also published when he was the feature poet of the month of the *Canadian Federation of Poets* at: http:// www.federationofpoets.com/featureraymondfenech.htm

Raymond designs custom-made courses in various writing disciplines for both adults and children. These include creative writing courses in poetry, fiction, article and short story writing and basic programmes in journalism, copywriting and PR. Course information is available on his web site: www.write-right.info

Recently, the author was appointed an Associate Editor with both *Adelaide Literary Magazine* and their Book Publishing House which has offices in both Lisbon and New York.

He is currently working on four books: his memoirs, *Forgotten Fairy-tales; The Benefits of Creative Writing;* a novel, *The Vampire of Peaceville;* and the memoirs of Malta's top veterinary surgeon.

His poetry now forms part of the master's degree in the creative writing programme, at Holguin University in Cuba.

A POET IS BORN
By Dr Raymond Fenech

I have undertaken several poetry writing courses and from experience this question is highly controversial. Some will say that one can learn how to write poetry, whilst others will tell you that a poet is born.

I was practically born with the pen in my hand. At 8 in Primary School, I started writing compositions that were highly imaginative, to the point one day my teacher sent a note to my parents asking them not to do the homework for me. From there on, I never looked back. My writing capabilities became evident but my parents were more concerned I would have problems finding a job if I chose the arts. In secondary school, I was basically forced to choose sciences and until the very last year, it still looked as if I would pursue my studies in marine biology.

Then one day, the inevitable happened. I was 13 and my English teacher, Kay Cardona called me aside after the lesson. A couple of days before, I had submitted my homework, which consisted of an essay called, *Snowstorm.* Basically, what she had to say was that perhaps I should reconsider taking up sciences when I seemed so talented in writing.

It took me a night and a day to decide, but 24 hours after speaking with my teacher, I faced my parents and announced I intended to skip a year of college in order to be able to catch up with my art subjects, as this was my true vocation.

Another thing to be taken into consideration, at 14 my sister took me with her to her singing lessons. She was a *mezzo soprano.* Jokingly she asked her teacher, a very local famous opera singer to test my voice. I will never forget the embarrassment. It took them a long time to persuade me to do this exercise. At first, I was shy and at one point, I actually managed to follow the music teacher's precise instructions and started to follow the tune she played on her piano. When she heard me sing, she would not let me go. She said I was a naturally gifted baritone and having such a voice at such a young age was very promising. But I did not really want to become a professional opera singer. The determination to become a writer was so strong that to this day, I can never figure out how I managed to choose writing instead of singing.

This decision was probably the most important of my budding career as a writer. From that moment on, I was about to learn the first lesson of what it takes to be a writer and a poet. My parents threw everything they had at me, saying that I was going to fail in my mission and that choosing writing as a career was as possible as wishing to travel to the moon. But my mind was set and even at 14, I was determined not to let anyone, or anything deter me from my dream.

It was a difficult dream at that time because not only careers, or openings for writers in my country were non-existent, but the country was under the Mintoffian regime. Malta was a police-run state. The prime minister of that time, Mintoff was all out to discourage people

from pursuing professional careers, especially in journalism. He was all out to suffocate freedom of thought and freedom of speech, as well as freedom of press.

When I went to the University of Malta, to enquire about the journalism course, which I thought was the closest and only thing I could enrol for to practice my writing, I was told the course had been abolished by the Government as it was considered, as not required.

There were no options really, but to seek some other profession, or study journalism through correspondence. The journalism course I chose was conducted by a UK based professional body. I was bombarded by my family but by hook or by crook, my mind was set to finish what I had started.

When I returned from the UK, I started to freelance for three major political newspapers and after a year, was called for an interview with Malta's leading English newspapers, *The Times* and *Sunday Times.* The event was a determining move in my career. The offices of the newspaper I was joining had just been attacked and gutted by Socialist thugs, part of the Mintoffian regime. It was a frightening move and many people raised eyebrows when I told them that I had taken the job. From that moment on, despite great difficulties and gruelling times ahead that saw me safely through some dangerous situations, I never looked back.

In the meantime, I had never stopped writing poetry. Some of it was amateurish, because I had never really received any guidance or training. There were no poetry writing courses at that time and no internet. The important thing is that I never stopped. I read all the poetry books I could get my hand on and learnt how to write the hard way – by trial and error. However, I still managed to publish a poem here and there and won the odd poetry prize as well, albeit the competitions were

not major ones, but mostly organised by small press publications. Still, these small successes kept me going and hoping.

This was another important phase, because I learnt that determination and perspiration were as important as inspiration. Now, I realised why other budding poets in my time failed and gave up hope of ever becoming published poets. I never aspired to become famous, kept my feet solidly on the ground and just kept reading, writing and sending out poems. There were editors who gave me good advice, others said things which were discouraging and some never even bothered to answer my submissions, no not even with a standard rejection slip. After all, who was this alien from nowhere who was expecting his work to be reviewed, never mind published. But even all this negativeness and discouragement taught me the most important thing - to distinguish between constructive and destructive criticism. This helped me to move on. Writing poetry is like playing football – you have to keep the ball moving, otherwise you lose tempo and the ball to the opposition.

I spent a small fortune on several leading poetry publishing directories and spent hours studying the market, always trying to find journals, or magazines that suited my style of poetry. I spent a fortune on postal stamps, envelopes, International Reply Coupons, as I often made multiple submissions to increase the chances of acceptance. Well the acceptances started to come instead of the rejection slips I had become so accustomed to.

However, I was still not happy and by now, poetry writing courses were sprouting everywhere. I undertook several writing courses with *The Writing School,* the *Open College of the Arts* and *Thames Valley University,* the *Institute of Copywriting* and *Stonebridge Associated Colleges.* I think I must have been one of the first to

have a computer and internet service in Malta. Of course, internet facilitated my work and I was soon adding more publishing credits to my list.

I believe that writing is a vocation. I don't think it is ideal for the faint hearted, or for people who would rather undertake a profession that brings money and success very quickly. Lawyers, doctors and businessmen surely are much better off when it comes to their annual salaries than writers. Poetry writing, more than writing fiction can be a very slow and painful road to the top. And few are talented or determined enough to reach the top. From the experiences I've been through, I have also noted that unfortunately we live in a world where what you know does not really matter – sometimes it's who you know that really counts. I have read poetry that is not worth the paper it's been printed on and yet because the writer's name is well known, it is given prominence in leading literary magazines, or anthologies.

To become a better writer I utilize Nathalie Goldberg's, *Rules of Writing* in her book, *Wild Mind – Living the Writer's Life.* There are seven rules and I consider them as if they were the seven commandments for all budding poets.

Ms Goldberg's advice to writers in her Rule 1 is described by Peter Sansom in his book, *Writing Poems, (Bloodaxe Poetry Handbook: 2)* as Free Writing is often also referred to as Hot-penning. This exercise is excellent, especially as a warm-up session. In order to obtain the best results, one must start writing without stopping and most important of all, without thinking. The writer must let the writing take its own route, and as far away as possible from what Ms Goldberg describes as, *The Editor.*

I often use this method when I need to loosen up my mind and to break away from conventional thinking. It

helps a great deal to solve the common problem of *Writer's Block*. Personally, I think that some of my best poems came about thanks to this method.

Having designed creative writing courses for both adults and children, I have found it most suitable to give the class a sentence, or a single line, example: *In the distance ...,* from which students are then invited to continue writing. I have found it helpful to clear one's mind before embarking on this exercise and to avoid rhyming the words - that is unless this happens naturally in the process.

Rule no 2 recommended by Goldberg is of utmost importance because it is truly difficult for any writer, especially a beginner to write openly. What Ms Goldberg advises is for the writer to lose control. Usually, when a writer writes he tends to think about what he is writing. This often reduces the impact of an original piece and can kill creativity and the genius that it can give to a piece of good writing. This also increases the danger, which Goldberg warns against, *The Editor.* *The Editor* in the writer creates another danger, which comes in the form of too much editing and re-writing. *Authenticity*, as Goldberg describes it, is often based on the courage to write and to say whatever one really feels. Which reminds me about my favourite poet, John Keats' most brilliant dictum: *"Poetry must work out its own salvation in a man, it cannot be matured by law and precept, but by sensation and watchfulness in itself. That which is creative must create itself."*

Losing control is one of the ingredients required in the recipe to produce some of the finest artistic creations, be it poetry, painting or music. Eliot once said: *"The bad poet is usually unconscious where he ought to be conscious, and conscious where he ought to be unconscious."* There is nothing like losing control for one to be creative and truthful in what one writes.

When I resort to this rule, I force myself to be honest and sum up enough courage to say things the way I feel and see them, without any kind of censorship. I am very much aware that this procedure has its drawbacks and that it has hurt the career of many writers, for the simple reason that characters and situations are often easily recognised, or identified by the persons they are referring to. However, the advantages supersede the disadvantages and most of the writers that suffered, in the long run found that the sacrifice paid off.

Goldberg's Rule 3 actually sent me back a few decades and reminded me when I embarked on my journalistic career. Actually, I consider this the rule of rules because paying attention to detail could make the difference between a great news story worthy of the front page, or a mediocre article that would appear as a filler in some remote corner of the newspaper. When writing, whether it is a journalistic article, a poem or a short story, detail could make all the difference. I have found this out through personal experience, because readers often tell me that they often associate themselves with a situation, an experience, or character in an article or a story. This fact compels them to read on, contrary to when an inexperienced writer bores them to death and proves that he has no idea about what he is talking about. Most often these articles lack detail and when detail is lacking, so is the realistic feeling.

Rule 4, *Don't Think* is easier said than done. The mind does follow a process of first and second thoughts and it's difficult to disengage oneself from this basic procedure. I cannot but agree with Goldberg when she insists that a writer should stay with the first flash. Having worked as a journalist, proof reader and editor for so many years, using this process for me proved much more difficult. However, after constant practice,

the procedure became much easier to handle, even if I have to confess, the editor in me at times takes over momentarily before I realise and cast him away.

When I sit down to do some hot-penning, I try to clear my mind of any pending thoughts, except for the flash that appears like a light bulb at the end of the mind's dark tunnel. The light intensifies and I find my hand being guided by the ghost in the ink pot. It's a marvellous feeling of relaxation that gives the mind the opportunity to be free from the daily routine thoughts and gives vent to creativity.

Rule 5 is very important because it subtends rules 1, 2 and 4. If the writer stops to edit punctuation, the magic of free writing will be lost. I apply this rule in the same manner as I apply rule 4. The hand must be left free to follow the light of the flash that appears in the dark tunnel of the mind. Rule 5 also brings to my mind a statement made by Adrienne Rich: *"Poems are like dreams, in them you put what you don't know you know."*

French poet Apollinaire was often criticised because he wrote poems without using any punctuation. So I figure if he can do it and go on to become famous, why shouldn't other poets follow his example? Should punctuation be required in any given piece of work? A poet always has ample time to edit and re-write whatever would have come out of the mysterious tunnel of the brain. This form of poetic licence must create an effect.

After experimenting in a 20-minute free writing exercise, I often find myself doubting if the writer of that piece of writing was actually me. If I had any doubts about people having dual personalities, now I don't. This is precisely the purpose that Goldberg recommends this rule. It gives vent not only to creativity, but to the subconscious mind, allowing its genius to come to the fore. This is how most of the greatest works of art have come about.

Rule 6 is an added ingredient to the idea of free writing. Following the flash, often brings up unpredictable subjects, or themes that are not always a priority in our stereo-typed minds. Too often we brush these ideas aside, thinking that they are junk, as Goldberg describes them. However, writers often prefer to describe that which they are afraid to write about as rubbish, when in truth, that rubbish could prove to be the basis to a best selling piece.

For example, how many writers would be willing to write about their own sexual fantasies or tendencies? Their first worry would be, what others will think of them – their boss, their parents, their wife or fiancée, friends and even the green grocer from whom they do their weekly shopping. How many writers would actually put pen to paper and write about their family problems, the abuse they suffered from their parents when they were children, the alcoholic problem which their father managed to hide from the rest of the world for so long, the rape of one of their close relatives, which remained a secret, even though it resulted in an illegitimate child being put away in an orphanage, or being aborted to keep the family name and reputation intact?

Goldberg advises writers to write about anything that is under the sky, and if this is junk they should feel free to write about it. But they can also write about the forbidden secrets of their family, their inner most secrets, sexual trends, or their hate for religion and conventionalism, which was forced down their throats since they were still children.

When I write, I try to write about everything that is under the sun without mincing words. I try not to be conventional and keep away from the influence of the Church, religion and politics, as well as the parochialism

that hems in and hampers the community I live in. I take flight on invisible wings and go beyond the cage which harnesses my intelligence and the thirst for transparency and knowledge. It has taken me a long time to break free from these chains, that have weighed me down for so long. Now, I can safely say, I have outgrown the arrogance and ignorance which both political and Church institutions indulge in and propagate among the population in order to be able to keep overall control.

Rule 7, *Go for the jugular* is a massive commitment and probably the toughest test for any writer. I can recount an incident, which I remember when I did just that some years ago. I was invited to a very rare poetry reading. I had just published a small book of poems. The reading took place at a local theatre and I was very excited about it all. The organisers decided to choose one of my poems called, Broken Innocence. The poem speaks about the first love and sexual experience shared by two thirteen-year old kids who were cousins. The poem is very vivid and the crowd did not applaud at the end of the reading. The reaction was silence and softly spoken remarks, which from what I could discern definitely showed disapproval. The poem had worked because it had done exactly what it was intended to do, stun the public with a reality few would have had the courage to speak about never mind write. I was pleased, but writing about real events, people and oneself comes at a very costly price. However, if this brings so much satisfaction, then it's all worthwhile.

Writing about what really hurts is more likely to produce the best ingredients for a good poem. A credible piece of writing has to bleed in order to move readers to tears or laughter and to do this, one has to write in blood. Ingredients for this type of writing can only come from personal experience. For example, I find it most painful to write about cancer. I fear to thread on the subject

because it brings back horrid memories of acute pain, suffering and even death. Almost three years passed without my touching on the subject, yet I knew that one day I was going to have to face that fear and write about it. The time has come, because I have just started writing a novel called, *The Vampire of Peaceville.* The story is based on personal experience and recounts the story of a young executive who is diagnosed with terminal cancer at the peak of his career. He lives in constant fear of his frail health and this puts him in touch with the paranormal. He suddenly becomes obsessed with the cravings of immortality and starts to see the world around him from a complete different perspective. One day, he meets with a real vampire who not only befriends him, but offers him a complete recovery from his cancer. Although his illness becomes a thing of the past, so does his mortal body. A metamorphosis has taken place and he must now embark into a new world as a creature of the night, a vampire. The description of my chemo sessions have come into extremely good use, but the pain is greater now than it was during the actual administration of the medicine.

Earlier, I mentioned reading as one of the most important ingredients a poet needs to do, in order to become a good poet. I have come across budding poets that tell me they are not interested in reading poetry. If they don't read other poets' works, how can they expect their poems to interest other writers? It's a vicious circle. What goes around comes around.

"The first skill of any writer is the skill to read," says poet, critic and managing director of Carcanet Press, Michael Schmidt. Peter Sansom writes in his chapter on *Reading* in his book, *Writing Poems*, that *"Reading poetry is a skill that many, even published writers never acquire of all the variables that come into play here, and that the quality of one's writing reflects*

the quality of one's reading." (Bloodaxe Poetry Handbooks: 2).

Since I was a child, I have always been taught, reading books helped to improve one's writing skills and imagination. My parents were adamant to see to it that I would become an avid reader. My father and my elder sister read whole books in a single day. My father used to insist reading was the only way to learn, not only grammar, but also the spoken language. He insisted that books gave one an education and knowledge no academic institution could possibly match. We did not have a television then and that was a good thing, because the only ways of entertainment, especially during the wintry seasons, or the long summer holidays were reading good books. The classics were the best to start off with, such as *Twenty Thousand Leagues Under the Sea, "Robinson Crusoe", Treasure Island, Ivanhoe, Gulliver's Travels, The Portrait of Dorian Grey* and many more. So, most of the gifts I received for my birthday and Christmas, consisted of books.

At school, I studied three languages besides Maltese and reading books really gave me an advantage over other students, especially when it came to both writing impeccably and enhancing my vocabulary knowledge. Reading for writers is a must. No writer can become a professional, unless he is prepared to invest hours in reading. I remember when I was still at primary school, I was an avid reader of *The Famous Five* and *The Secret Seven* books by Eynid Blyton. One day I wrote a composition, which my English teacher had given me as homework. After she read it, she wrote to my parents and asked them not to help me with my homework. The truth was, I had done my homework alone, but the influence and knowledge obtained from the books I read made my composition seem too good to have been written by an eight year old. My parents spoke to my

teacher, and after, she never doubted my writing capability again.

However, I strongly believe from there on, the writer in me was born, and since then I have never looked back. Reading inevitably gives writers fresh knowledge and ideas. Often, after reading a poem, I would write one myself. If it's not a complete poem, I pick words, or a phrase that attracts my attention and use it for a free writing session. The results are very surprising and sometimes even mind boggling.

Reading other writers helps to develop a strong sense of constructive criticism. I always think the worse criticism I get for my own work is from me. So, it helps when other fellow writers or editors read my work and give me a positive reaction. It's encouraging. It would be extremely boring to read only one's own work. I read mine many times, only when I create it, edit and proofread it. Then it's the readers who have to judge, because after, I hardly ever touch it again, unless one of my editors recommends changes.

Professional writers and poets can teach readers, or fellow writers several tricks of the trade. When it comes to poetry, these tricks are even more obvious and one can emulate the writer by adapting the same trick, using it in his own work. The importance of detail in descriptions, whether poetic or prose was something I learnt from reading. In fact, a lot of the tricks of the trade I learnt came from sheer observation when reading some of the master writers such as, Ernest Heminway, Franz Kafka, Scott Fitzgerald, Somerset Maugham and my two favourite poets, John Keats and Pablo Neruda. I learnt how to write visual poetry after I read Apollinaire. So yes, reading other writers is as important as writing itself. Last but not least, poets must remember, buying books generates business in the publishing industry, thus encouraging publishers to publish more. It is no use

complaining about the lack of interest from readers, because these aren't buying enough books when we, who should be setting the example do the same.

Write your piece, leave it for a couple of days, then go back to it. Don't try to edit and complete it as soon as you have made the first draft. If you do, you risk losing its artistic value. Return to edit as many times as you deem necessary, but one thing is for certain, NEVER submit a new work as soon as you finish writing it. You will regret it, because you will be bound to read it again at some point and discover you could have produced a finer piece had you left it for a while before editing.

Earlier I wrote about *losing control* and to appeal to the unconscious in order to produce the magic in one's poetry or prose. When writing, one must let his fancy flow and follow his instinct. The attitude and the emotion here must be free to roam the debts of the unconscious mind, so it can give vent to creativity.

Editing is a very important support service to one's creativity, but it must be done at the appropriate time, sparingly and with great diligence. Editing can actually harm a very good piece of work, because some writers have a tendency to over edit, until the edited article is only a shadow of the original. It happened to me very often in the past. Writers must learn to be God and the devil at the same time.

Writing poetry has to consist of the process of letting out one's wrath, going berserk and stripping naked in front of an audience, showing both one's ugly inner and outer parts and the truth, no matter how painful or scandalous.

Editing is the part when the writer is back to his normal self, in his senses, fully aware and ready to correct grammatical, orthographical mistakes and apply punctuation. Editing has to be undertaken with great scruples and as Goldberg recommends trying not to be

too hard on oneself. I have often ruined poems because the editor in me takes complete control and goes on a merciless rampage, often massacring poetic lines which would have made the work very special. For this reason, it is best to always keep the original scripts. It's a sort of counter action against the carnage which the editor in the writer can cause.

To become a better poet, I have also often resorted to my own life experiences to provide material for my writing. This inevitably brings to mind a quotation by Jean Rostand, which I read in a book called, *The Courage to Write,* by Ralph Keyes. Rostand defines literature as, *proclaiming in front of everyone what one is careful to conceal from one's immediate circle.* The best ever written literature has come directly from stories based mostly on the authors' personal life experiences. Chaucer's *Canterbury Tales* were based on true characters and experiences, as were the characters depicted by the Marquis de Sade. Ernest Hemmingway wrote most of his stories, basing them on true life characters he met during his extraordinary travels, as did Somerset Maugham, John Steinbeck, and John Fitzgerald. Poets like Baudelaire, Apollinaire, Alessandro Manzoni, Giacomo Leopardi, Foscolo, Patricia Beer and the master of spy books, creator of 007, Ian Fleming, all wrote basing their master pieces on their own true life experiences. For example, Fleming formed part of the British Secret Service for many years.

I remember that at the very beginning of my career, a certain editor of a magazine had asked me to write an article. When I asked him what I should write about, he simply answered me saying: *The best is to write about a subject you know about and have had hands on experience.* In fact most of my poems, articles, short stories and research are based on personal experience. Most have remained indelible in my memory because

they have caused me pain, discomfort, embarrassment, joy, laughter or anger and fear.

The novel I am working on at the moment, *The Vampire of Peaceville* though a fictitious composition, is based on true happenings. The vampire goes through the difficult period of facing terminal illness, chemotherapy, the frustration of seeing his career, which is at its very peak come to an inevitable end, and facing up to the humiliation of finding himself in financial difficulties and jobless. All these ingredients are taken from my own personal life experiences as an ex-cancer survivor.

Not only, but now I am finding out that it is equally difficult for a cancer survivor to maintain certain privileges within his community, which he had before succumbing to this illness. For example, ask any cancer survivor what the chances are of finding a job? Cancer is like a death sentence, which kills you even if you survive through it. Opportunities, career-wise are hard to come by. Even if cancer patients survive, the constant fear that their illness could return at some stage in their lives, will force them to discover at their own expense that a more difficult hurdle to surmount is right in their own back yard, in their own imminent surroundings. I have learnt that bank loans are a difficult thing to obtain after one falls victim to cancer, as is a health insurance cover. Most of my clients left me during my illness, not because I had become inefficient, but for fear that I would succumb to the illness and they would be left with incomplete advertising campaigns.Surely this experience will serve me well and one day, I might write a poem or an article about it, who knows? Never mind finding a job – every employer is scared stiff even at the mere mention of the word cancer. It's like you have mentioned Lucifer and that you are one of his servants!

I have never had doubts, even before I embarked on my writing career, that most successful writers based

their stories on true accounts and personal experiences. For a reader, it is easy to note this because when reading a book, he will find many instances when he would be assimilating his own experiences to those of one of the characters created by the authors.

As a poet and a writer I have also enjoyed moments of discovering myself.

When I started writing I never realised that not only I was embarking on one of the most exhilarating experiences of my life, but that I would discover myself, my true nature and all my capabilities, creative and otherwise. The first thing I discovered was whether I was a courageous person or not, and to what extent I was determined to succeed as a writer.

The first time I discovered I was very determined was when at 13, I returned home from school and announced to my perplexed parents that I wanted to change from sciences to arts. To say that my parents were shocked would be an understatement. I remember I was called several names, including a failure, dreamer, bull headed, looser, irresponsible and quite a few more adejectives, but still I was adamant to maintain my course. My determination to become a writer was such that no amount of arguing, threatening, or cajoling could derail me from my new found vocation. I had set my mind to start off as a journalist and I was prepared to do anything to achieve my goal.

I endured a lot of flack from my family in the months that followed but this made me even more resolute. The first opportunity for me came from a local political English newspaper, *The Democrat*. I was offered a post as a junior correspondent apprenticed to the newspaper's editor. It wasn't much, but I was still 17 and raring to go and on top of that determined to prove to my parents that I was right all along to choose this

career and that I could succeed. At that age, I had no experience of Parliamentary reporting, but I just couldn't turn down my very first opportunity. Malta was then being run by the Mintoffian regime and democracy and freedom of speech. Reporting for an opposition newspaper was like working as a war correspondent. I had undertaken a six-month journalism course, but this hardly covered the danger or stressful conditions of work which I was to face in the coming years. It was during this time, I discovered I was a great optimist and a quick decision maker. This phase in my life was a preparation for more difficult times to come.

Trying to be a poet was another relentless challenge that was not easy to overcome. In fact, I spent most of my time struggling to surmount the most difficult hurdle – to manage to get a book of my poetry published by a recognised publisher. I was warned at the start of my career that many have attempted to publish their poetry, but only few succeeded.

Since there were no creative writing classes in my country, I had to teach myself this art. Poetry also helped me discover a lot of likes and dislikes. I identified the subjects I liked to write about, the style of writing I preferred and the kind of publications I enjoyed reading and eventually submitting work to. I also learnt how to tolerate and handle, arrogant and unhelpful editors, who had serious attitude problems. Writing also helped me discover that I was a hypersensitive person and realised that what I had always thought as being a weakness, instead was actually one of the greatest assets for inspiration. It was a very important part of the recipe, which helped me become a published writer.

Writing has even improved my sense of choice, judgement and brought out an aggressiveness and courage I never thought I possessed. I am sure that there is still a lot more to discover about myself in future,

given the time. But the strangest of things was how inspiration descends quickly upon me and that unless I catch it on the spot, no matter where I am, I lose the poem that I believe is being channelled to me.

Channelling to paranormal investigators means receiving information from the beyond. I realized this because whenever I was struck by one of these transcendent states, I wrote fast without even knowing the meaning of what I was writing. The words came, fitted in between each line like a glove, in perfect synchronization, without my even having to make any effort whatsoever. To say that the end result of each of these poems was a miracle would be an understatement. And all the poems that came to me in this manner, at the oddest hours of the day, when sometimes I was already half asleep, even in a sort of daze, were the best I ever wrote. Then, the most peculiar thing would be reading the poem back and discovering that this came out of nowhere, was in my humble opinion a perfectly finished article, and had written this so well in few seconds, when compared to other poems which took months and sometimes years to complete

Becoming a poet can be a true wonderful journey as one recognizes the very essence of life. Unfortunately, writing poetry can be a gruelling experience, but the long term achievements are ever so rewarding that if I were to be reborn, I would do exactly the same things all over again, except perhaps give up singing. I think I could have coped with both writing and becoming a professional opera singer.

Dr. Raymond Fenech

Acknowledgements

The Dream and the Glory: a) The Adelaide Literary Magazine, USA, Year II No. 7 Vol 1, June 2017; b) Envoy, Official Newsletter of the Canada Cuba Literary Alliance Issue No. 076, August 2016, Cuba

The Swing in the Garden: a) The Adelaide Literary Magazine Year III, Number 9, Vol. Two, USA, September 2017; b) Father/Grandfather Anthology 2013 by Reflections of the Past is a division of Hidden Brook Publishers, Canada; c) Boston Poetry Magazine, USA, 2014

The Green Boat: a) The Ambassador Vol. 2017 by the Canada Cuba Literary Alliance, Canada; b) Boston Poetry Magazine, USA, 2014; c) Borderless Skies (Cielo Sin Fronteras), Anthology by the Canada Cuba Literary Alliance, 2007

Ave Maria: a) Forever Friends Anthology, Triumph House Publishers, UK, 1999; b) Teak Roundup VII, Canada, 1997

Growing With the Shadows: a) Poemata Issue 11, the main poetry journal of the Canadian Poetry Association, Canada, 2000; b) Verses Magazine, USA, 2003; c) Poetry Canada (Print Version) Issue December/January/February, 2006

The Primary School Classroom: a) Once Upon A Story Time Anthology, Anchor Books, UK 2001; b) Once Upon A Story Time Anthology, Anchor Books, UK, 2000; c) Once Upon A Story Time Anthology, Anchor Books, UK 2000; d) Canada Cuba Literary Alliance Volunteer Anthology, The Banquet of the Now, 2009; e) Ygdrasil Online Magazine Issue 7, Canada, 2000; f) Linkway Magazine Issue 3, UK, 2005; g) Chrysalis Issue 4 Histories, UK, August 2013; h) Blood Lines Poetry Collection, SandCrab Books, Cuba, 2012.

Gladiolus: a) published under another name, The Sword Lily, Canada Cuba Literary Alliance Volunteer Anthology, The Banquet of the Now, 2009

My Great Aunt's house in Zejtun: a) The Ambassador Vol. 10, the Canada Cuba Literary Alliance, Canada, 2011; b) Linkway Magazine Issue, UK, 2005; b) Breakfast All Day Quarterly Issue 13, France, 1999; c) Reality Of Life Anthology, Poetry Now Publishers, UK, 2001; d) The Crossroads Of Life Anthology, Anchor Books, UK, 2000; e) The Ambassador Vol. 10, the Canada Cuba Literary Alliance, Canada, 2011; f) Poetry Heaven Online Magazine 4: USA, 2000

A Grain of Sand in Reflections: a) Verse Anthology, Anchor Books, UK 2001; b) Third Half Magazine, Issue 36 published by K.T. Publications, UK, 2003

240

An Apology to Pooch (1999-2011): a) Blood Lines, SandCrab Books, Cuba, 2012

Death of a Stray Cat: a) Saolpeot, The Quarterly Magazine of the Salopian Poetry Society Issue   No.158, Winter, UK, 2015.

In Memoriam To Rex I: a) poem was published under the title, "In Memoriam: To an Irish Setter", The Wonder of Animals, Poetry Now Publishers, UK, 2003; b)Two By Two Anthology, Arrival Press, UK, 1997, c) George Pope Morris, an Anthology in Memoriam, USA, 2002; d) Solar Voice No.2 UK, October, 2001

This will never happen to me Syndrome: a) The Adelaide Literary Magazine Year III, Number 9, Vol. Two, USA, September 2017

To Sadness: a) The Adelaide Literary Magazine, Year II No. 7 Vol 1, USA, June 2017; b) Envoy, Official Newsletter of the Canada Cuba Literary Alliance Issue No. 076, Cuba, August 2016

The Waiting Room: a) The Adelaide Literary Magazine, Year II No. 7, Vol 1, USA, June 2017, b) Blood Lines, poetry collection SandCrab Books, Cuba, 2012; c) White Ash Literary Magazine, USA 2017, d) Salopeot, The Quarterly Magazine of the Salopian Poetry Society Issue No.161, Autumn UK, 2016

The Glory and the Strife: a) The Envoy, Issue 080 the official newsletter of the Canada Cuba Literary Alliance, 2017

A Sonnet with Some Advice: a) Troubled Times Anthology, Triumph house Publishers, UK, 1996, b) Salopeot, the Quarterly Magazine of the Salopian Poetry Society Issue No. 162, Winter UK, 2016

Operation – Travelling Towards the Light: a) Captured thought Anthology, Triumph House Publishers, UK, 2000; b) Salopeot, The Quarterly Magazine of the Salopian Poetry Society, Issue No. 154 Winter, UK, 2014; c) Verses Magazine XI, USA, 1999

When Death Came to Visit, White Ash Literary Magazine, USA, 2017; b) Envoy, Official Newsletter of the Canada Cuba Literary Alliance Issue No. 076, August 2016, Cuba

In Memoriam to my Father (1920-1994): a) Richard Hovey an Anthology in Memoriam, Bristol Banner Books, USA, 2000; b) Canada Cuba Literary Alliance, Volunteer Anthology, The Banquet of the Now, 2009; c) Poets Review Online 8, Canada, 2000; d) Crystal Magazine Issue 12, November, UK, 2002; e) Blood Lines poetry collection, Sand Crab Books, Cuba, 2012

The Straw Hat: a) Time Stood Still Anthology, Anchor Books, UK, 2000: b) Windfall Canadian Poetry Anthology for Members, Hidden Brook Press, Canada, 2002, c) Blood Lines poetry collection, SandCrab Books, Cuba, 2012; d) The Affectionate Punch IX, UK, 1999; e) Poetic Licence 18, Poets Anonymous, UK, 2002; f) Other Poetry, UK, 2003; g) Quantum Leap May Issue No 22, Scotland, 2003; h) Third Half Magazine, Issue 36 published by K.T. Publications, UK 2003; i) Boston Poetry Magazine, USA, 2014; j) White Ash Literary Magazine Issue 4, To the Moon and Back, USA, 2014; k) Salopeot, The Quarterly Magazine of the Salopian Poetry Society Issue No. 155, Spring, UK, 2015; l) The Adelaide Literary Magazine Year III, Number 9, Vol. Two, September 2017, USA; m) The Ambassador, Vol. 004, published by the Canada Cuba Literary Alliance, 2006

The Mannequin: a) Quail Bell Magazine, USA Issue May, 2017

Light After Dark: a) The Future Looks Bright (The Canadian Federation of Poets, Members' Anthology), Canada, 2005; b) Count Our Blessings by forward Press, UK, 2007; c) Linkway Magazine Issue, UK, 2005; d) Flaming Arrows Issue 8, Flaming Arrows Publications, Ireland, 2005; e) White Ash Literary Magazine Issue 5, Onyx, USA, 2015; f) Salopeot, The Quarterly Magazine of the Salopian Poetry Society Issue No.160, Summer, UK, 2016; g) The Adelaide Literary Magazine Year III, Number 9, Vol. Two, USA, September 2017

Inside the Bare Wall: a) Maurice Thompson the Early Years, an Anthology in Memoriam (1844-1901), Bristol Banner Books, USA, 2001; b) Poets Review Online 8, Canada, 2000; c) Flaming Arrows, Flaming Arrows Publishers, Ireland, 2002; d) Rebirth No. 6, UK, 2002; d) Third Half Magazine, Issue 36, K.T. Publications, UK, 2003

On Imagination: a) A Tapestry Of Thoughts, a special anthology, Spotlight Poets, UK, 1998; b) The Solar Voice No. 5, the New Renaissance, UK, 2002

The Dancing Bag: a) Expressions Online Magazine, Canada, December issue, 2005

The Ghost in the Ink Pot: a) Rebirth No. 6, UK, 2002; b) ImageNation Vol 3, Jan 30 Edition, UK, 2003

Platonic Love: a) The Adelaide Literary Magazine Year III, Number 9, Vol. Two, September, USA, 2017; b) EskimoPi online Magazine, USA, 2017

Fleur: a) The Ambassador, Vol. 9, the Canada Cuba Literary Alliance, Canada, 2010; b) The Adelaide Literary Magazine Year III, Number 9, Vol. Two, September, USA, 2017; c) Blood Lines, poetry collection, SandCrab Books, Cuba, 2012

Our Maid Claire: a) The Adelaide Literary Magazine Year III, Number 9, Vol. Two, September, USA, 2017

Forbidden Love: a) The Envoy, Issue 080 the official newsletter of the Canada Cuba Literary Alliance, Canada, 2017; b) The Adelaide Literary Magazine, USA, Year II No. 7 Vol 1, 2017

Endless Love: a) Blood Lines, poetry collection, SandCrab Books, Cuba, 2012

Broken Innocence: a) Boston Poetry Magazine, USA, 2014; b) Blood Lines, poetry collection, SandCrab Books, Cuba, 2012

Bovary: a) Poet's Paradise V, USA, 1997; b) Teak Roundup X, Canada, 1998; c) Second Time Single Anthology, Poetry Now Publishers, UK, 1993

The Girl on the Gozo Ferry Boat: a) Shifting Sands Anthology, Anchor Books, UK, 1994; b) Dusting Of Dreams Anthology, Quill Books, USA, 1995; c) Thought Magazine Issue 4, USA, 2002; d) Blood Lines, poetry collection, SandCrab Books, Cuba, 2012

The Dandelion Seed (Petrarchan Sonnet): a) Envoy, Official Newsletter of the Canada Cuba Literary Alliance Issue No. 076, Cuba, 2016; b) The Adelaide Literary Magazine Year III, Number 9, Vol. Two, September, USA

Poppies are Not Even in Dreams, White Ash Literary Magazine, USA, 2017

A Mosquito's Buzzing Birth: a) Mirrored Souls Anthology, Poetry Now Publishers, UK, 2002; b) Borderless Skies (Cielo Sin Fronteras) Anthology, The Canada Cuba Literary Alliance, 2007; c) Blood Lines poetry collection, SandCrab Books, Cuba, 2012; d) Electric Acorn Issue 12, (Dublin Writers Workshop), Ireland, 2002; e) Dandelion Arts Magazine, December Issue, UK, 2002; f) Verses Magazine, USA, 2003; g) Dandelion Arts Magazine Issue 32, USA, 2003; h) Carillon, Issue 7 June 2003, UK; i) Third Half Magazine, Issue 36 published by K.T. Publications, UK, 2003; j) Boston Poetry Magazine, USA, 2014; k) White Ash Literary Magazine Issue 4, To the Moon and Back, USA, 2014; l) Salopeot, The Quarterly Magazine of the Salopian Poetry Society Issue No.159, Spring, UK, 2016; m) The Adelaide Literary Magazine Year III, Number 9, Vol. Two, September, USA 2017

Cobwebs: a) A Tapestry Of Thoughts: a) Spotlight Poets, UK, 1998; b) Paul Laurence Dunbar an Anthology in Memoriam (1872-1906), Bristol Banner Books, USA, 1997; c) Breakfast All Day Quarterly VI, (7), 21 France, 1997; d) A-pos'tro-phe Poetry Journal III (11), USA, 1997; e) The Poet's

Pen Quarterly Journal of the Society Of American Poets XI, USA, 1998; f) Anthology Web Zine 4, USA, 1999; g) Outreach Connection Weekly Newspaper, (1) 11, Canada, 2000

The Electric Storm: a) Poets Of The 90's Anthology, Arrival Press Publishers, UK, 1996; b) The Banquet of the Now, Canada Cuba Literary Alliance Volunteer Anthology, 2009; c) Poetalk, a Poetry Journal of Bay Area Poets Coalition XX, USA, 1997; d) Poet's Paradise V, USA, 1997

The Failed Summit with the Rain: a) A Tapestry of Thoughts, Spotlight Poets Series, UK, 1998; b) The Poet's Pen Quarterly Journal of the Society Of American Poets XI (1), USA, 1998; c) The Raintown Review II, USA, 1998

The Mountains of Mourne (Ireland): a) Spirit of Humanity Anthology, Artists For A Better World International, USA, 2007; b) The Aurorean a Poetic Quarterly 1, USA, 1997; c) Poet's Paradise III, USA, 1996; d) Micropress Yates III, Australia, 1998; e) Beyond the Seventh Morning Anthology, Canada Cuba Literary Alliance, SandCrab Books, a Division of Hidden Brook Press, Cuba, 2013; f) The Globe Trotter Magazine III, 7 Malta, 2000; g) Juju Magazine IV, (9), Northern Ireland, 2000; f) Dandelion Arts Magazine Issue 33, UK, 2003

Bonjour St. Hippolyte (South of France): a) Poetic Evolution Anthology, Poetry Now Publishers, UK, 2002; b) Borderless Skies (Cielo Sin Fronteras) Anthology, Canada Cuba Literary Alliance, 2007; c) Expressions Online Magazine, December issue, Canada, 2005; d) Quantum Leap Issue 29, Scotland, 2005

Remnants of St. Julian's Village: a) Memories are Made of this Anthology, Forward Press, UK, 2008; b) White Ash Literary Magazine Issue 6 Rituals, USA, 2016; c) Salopeot, The Quarterly Magazine of the Salopian Poetry Society Issue no. 152 Summer, UK, 2014; d) Blood Lines poetry collection, SandCrab Books, Cuba, 2012

The Carob Tree: a) Thomas Mackellar an Anthology in Memoriam (1812-1899) Bristol Banner Books, USA, 1999

To St. Julian: a) Open Window III An International Anthology of Poetry, Hidden Brook Press, Canada, 2002; b) The Banquet of the Now, Canada Cuba Literary Alliance Volunteer Anthology 2009; c) Third Half Magazine, Issue 36 published by K.T. Publications, UK, 2003; d) Linkway Magazine, UK, 2005; e) Iota Magazine, issue 75, University of Gloucestershire, UK, 2006; f) Boston Poetry Magazine, USA, 2014; g) White Ash Literary Magazine Issue 6 Rituals, USA, 2016

Within the Edges of Mortality: a) Behind the Spade Anthology, Poetry Now Publishers, UK, 1994; b) This poem was translated into Italian by Notary

Vincenzo Maria Pellegrini and entitled Entro I Limiti Della Mortalita and published by, Agenzia Di Stampa Settinanale Nord Sud Press Agency II, (3), Sicily, 1988; c) Poetalk XVII, USA, 1993

Paul the Meticulous Fisherman: a) Poetry Rivals Collection, Forward Press, UK, 2009; b) Write Justified, the newsletter of the Professional Writers' Special Interest British Group MENSA, December issue, UK, 2008; c) EskimoPi online Magazine, July issue, USA, 2017; d) Blood Lines poetry collection, SandCrab Books, Cuba, 2012; e) The Adelaide Literary Magazine Year III, Number 9, Vol. Two, September 2017, USA

The Vegetable and Fruit Vendour: a) The Adelaide Literary Magazine, Year II No. 7 Vol 1, September issue, USA, 2017; The Envoy, Issue 080 the official newsletter of the Canada Cuba Literary Alliance, 2017

The Legend of Gomerino Palace: a) Inspired Lines Anthology, Anchor Books, UK, 1998; b) The Children's Poetry Companion, Triumph house Publishers, UK, 1999; c) Time for Rhyme III, Canada, 1996

The Legend of the Dogwood: a) Cherished Thoughts Anthology, Triumph House Publishers, UK, 1997; b) A Tale to Tell Anthology, Triumph house Publishers, UK, 2000; c) Edwin Markham, an Anthology in Memoriam (1852-1940), Bristol Banner Books, USA, 2002; d) Flaming Arrows VI, Flaming Arrows Publishers, Ireland, 1997; e) The Poet's Pen Quarterly Journal of the Society Of American Poets XI, USA, 1998; f) Micropress OZ II, Australia, 1999; g) A Bard Hair Day Vol 7 April 30, Edition 2002, Creative Partners Publishers, UK, 2002; h) Gabriel Issue 2 Spring, UK, 2003; i) Salopeot, The Quarterly Magazine of the Salopian Poetry Society Issue no. 153 Autumn, UK, 2014

A Biography: a) Frances Sargent Osgood – an Anthology in Memoriam (1811-1850), Bristol Banner Books, USA, 2001; b) Torture and Triumph Anthology, Scars Publications & Design, USA, 2002; c) Scars Publications & Design Website, USA, 2001; d) Thought Magazine Issue 4, USA, 2002; e) Verses Magazine, USA, 2003; f) Write Justified, the newsletter of the Professional Writers' Special Interest British Group MENSA, December issue, UK, 2008

Waves: a) The Quarterly Magazine of the Salopian Poetry Society Issue No. 163, Spring, UK, 2017

Jilted: a) The Quarterly Magazine of the Salopian Poetry Society Issue No. 163, Spring, UK, 2017

Innocence of Old: a) The Quarterly Magazine of the Salopian Poetry Society Issue No. 163, Spring, UK, 2017

Dr. Raymond Fenech

The Concrete Jungle: a) The Quarterly Magazine of the Salopian Poetry Society Issue No. 163, Spring, UK, 2017

Falling in Love: a) Amber Magazine 2 Canada 1997; b) Through the Headlines, Poetry Now Publishers, UK, 1994; Fire and Ice, Armadillo Poetry Press, USA, 1998; c) Blood Lines poetry collection, SandCrab Books, Cuba, 2012

Paying for Air: a) Through the Headlines, Poetry Now Publishers, UK, 1994; b) Amber Magazine 5, Canada, 1995; c) Writers Viewpoint VIII, UK, 1995; d) Teak Roundup III, Canada, 1995

Sensitivity: a) Thoughts for Today, Triumph Book Publishers, UK, 1995; b) Amber Magazine 1, Canada, 1994; b) Amber Magazine 4, Canada, 1995; c) Amber Magazine 10, Canada, 1996; d) A-pos`tro-phe Poetry Journal III, USA, 1997; e) Introspection Online Magazine XI, USA, 1997; f) Poet's Paradise VII, USA, 1997; g) Introspection Online XII, USA, 1997; h) Anthology Magazine 2, USA, 1998

The Silent City (Mdina): a) Amber Magazine 10, Canada, 1995; b) Teak Roundup VIII, Canada, 1998; c) Salopeot the Quarterly Magazine 9 of the Salopian Poetry Society, UK, 1998

The Beheading: a) The Aurorean, A Poetic Quarterly IV, USA, 1998; b) Third Half Magazine, Issue 36 published by K.T. Publications, UK, 2003; c) Blood Lines poetry collection, SandCrab Books, Cuba, 2012

The King of Sorrow: a) Salopeot, The Quarterly Magazine of the Salopian Poetry Society, Spring Issue No. 163, UK, 2017

11488084R00148

Printed in Germany
by Amazon Distribution
GmbH, Leipzig